Victoria Groves

Phonemic Awareness

Ready-to-Use
Lessons, Activities,
and Games

Second Edition

CORWIN
A SAGE Company

For information:

Corwin
A SAGE Company
2455 Teller Road
Thousand Oaks, California 91320
(800) 233-9936
Fax: (800) 417-2466
www.corwinpress.com

SAGE Ltd.
1 Oliver's Yard
55 City Road
London EC1Y 1SP
United Kingdom

SAGE India Pvt. Ltd.
B 1/I 1 Mohan Cooperative
Industrial Area
Mathura Road, New Delhi 110 044
India

SAGE Asia-Pacific Pte. Ltd.
33 Pekin Street #02-01
Far East Square
Singapore 048763

Printed in the United States of America

Library of Congress Cataloging-in-Publication Data

Scott, Victoria Groves.
Phonemic awareness: ready-to-use lessons, activities, and games/
Victoria Groves Scott.—2nd ed.
        p. cm.
Includes bibliographical references and index.
ISBN 978-1-4129-7214-7 (cloth)
ISBN 978-1-4129-7215-4 (pbk.)

    1. English language—Phonemics—Study and teaching (Elementary)—Activity programs—United States. 2. Learning disabled children—Education (Elementary)— United States. 3. Reading—Phonetic method—United States. 4. Reading (Elementary)— Whole-word method—United States. I. Title.

LB1573.3.S39 2009
372.46′5—dc22   2009004464

This book is printed on acid-free paper.

09   10   11   12   13   10   9   8   7   6   5   4   3   2   1

Acquisitions Editor:	David Chao
Editorial Assistant:	Brynn Saito
Production Editor:	Catherine M. Chilton
Copy Editor:	Amy Rosenstein
Typesetter:	C&M Digitals (P) Ltd.
Proofreader:	Doris Hus
Indexer:	Sylvia Coates
Cover Designer:	Rose Storey

Contents

Acknowledgments

Thanks to the many individuals, past and present, whom I have worked with at various P–12 schools, colleges, and universities. Your work and research has deepened my understanding of reading instruction and disability issues. A special thanks to Patti Flenthrope, Mary Ellen Wade, Kirsten Bruce, Linda Pape, Sue Diel, and Allison Fahsl. And to all of my students from preschool to graduate school, I get my inspiration from you.

I'd also like to acknowledge the work done by all of the teachers at Lincoln Elementary in McPherson, Kansas, for their help piloting these lessons, and Neva Edwards, principal, for her support during the research. I'd like to thank my editors David Chao and Brynn Saito for their help and support during the revisions for the second edition of this book.

This book would not have nearly the number of cute drawings without the work of Juli Dirks, former student, artist, and first-grade teacher. She drew more than 100 of the pictures contained in this book. I'd also like to thank my son Brydon for his contribution to the artwork for this book.

Corwin Press would like to thank the following reviewers:

Marta Ann Gardner
Los Angeles Unified School District

Sonia Trehan Kelly
Blue River Montessori School, Duxbury, MA

Wanda Mangum
Gwinnett County Public Schools

Margaret L. Miller
Martin Luther Elementary School

Gary L. Willhite
University of Wisconsin–La Crosse

About the Author

 **Victoria Groves Scott**, Ed.D., has been working in the field of special education for more than 20 years. She received her doctorate in special education from the University of Kansas in 1995. She is currently the Director of Assessment for Southern Illinois University Edwardsville (SIUE) and Professor of Special Education. Prior to her appointment at SIUE in 2001, Professor Scott was chair of the Department of Special Education at the Associated Colleges of Central Kansas. Although she is a professor by trade, she remains a teacher by heart. Dr. Scott received the Teaching Excellence Award from SIUE in 2006 and the 2006 Emerson Excellence in Teaching Award. Dr. Scott was chosen by her peers as the Kansas Council for Exceptional Children Outstanding Special Education Teacher of the Year for 1998 and also was awarded the Council for Exceptional Children Federation Award in 1999. She has conducted research in the areas of phonemic awareness, reading instruction, assistive technology, and assessment. Dr. Scott has published two additional peer-reviewed textbooks: *Practical Cases in Special Education for All Educators* (2006) and *Cases in Special Education Assessment* (2005).

Dedicated, as always, with love to my husband, Jim, my sons, Brydon and Jaxon, and my parents, Gayle and Nadine Groves. I also would like to thank Dr. Mary Konya Weishaar, colleague and fellow researcher, for her support and friendship.

Introduction

The revised edition of *Phonemic Awareness: Ready-to-Use Lessons, Activities, and Games* contains an updated collection of lessons for children in grades kindergarten through three or students in grades four through six who have difficulty reading. These activities are sequenced around particular phonemes or sounds, not skills such as identification, blending, rhyming, segmentation, deletion, and/or manipulation. Therefore, they can be used out of order. If so desired, teachers could reorganize the lessons and teach all of the lessons on identification first, then blending, and so on. If the lessons are reorganized, the teacher will need to replace the review at the beginning of the lesson by asking questions to activate the student's prior knowledge in order to build on what the student already knows.

Besides updated lessons, this book also contains revised pictures and graphics that make concepts clearer for the students. And an updated and revised overview of phonemic awareness in Chapters 1 and 2 incorporates current research relating to phonemic awareness and phonemic awareness instruction.

HOW TO USE THESE LESSONS ■

The lessons are constructed using a modified Madeline Hunter lesson plan design. Each lesson opens with a *Review*, in which the teacher activates the students' prior knowledge and gains student attention. Next, the teacher presents the *Preview*, or anticipatory set; this is a simple communication from the teacher to the students about what they will learn. The *Presentation* or *Instruction* is the most important component of the lesson. Content is taught and modeled during the presentation. Next, students will practice the skill during the *Guided Practice* and *Independent Practice* phase. Guided practice is done with teacher supervision, and independent practice is done unaided. Finally, the teacher will *Review* what has been taught and *Preview* what the students can look forward to in future lessons. The review and preview at the end of the lesson bring closure to the lesson (Hunter, 1982). However, there are many other successful designs for lesson planning. The International Reading Association and National Council of Teachers of English have developed joint standards on reading and literacy that can assist teachers as they incorporate these lessons into their curriculum.

This star indicates an activity for enrichment or for older children. These activities require either a larger vocabulary, higher level thinking skills, or reading. They are intended to be used after the lesson.

Occasionally you will find that the lesson calls for the teacher to write the letter associated with the sound on the board. Although this is not a phonemic awareness task, it bridges the gap between phonemic awareness and letter recognition.

The notation /_/ tells you to *say the sound*. For example, we will be working on the /Ssss/ sound. Not, we will be working on the letter s or the sound for the letter s. Do you hear the short vowel /e/ at the beginning when you say the name of the letter s? Say that letter again. We want to work on the sound that comes after the short /e/. That's why it is important to say the letter *sound*, not the letter *name*. It is important to model phonemes as much as possible and to maintain a phonemic focus!

I hope you will add words to the lessons from your own curriculum. This practice will make learning occur more quickly and connect this skill to meaningful reading.

1

Overview of Phonemic Awareness

IMPORTANCE ■

Phonemic awareness has been a topic of much consideration and research over the past 20 years. Indeed, in the last five years, almost every recognized education journal has had articles on phonemic or phonological awareness and its impact on reading. You may be asking yourself why. It seems that within the past 20 years, reading researchers have begun to agree that phonological processing accounts for much of the variability in children's reading acquisition (Anthony, Williams, McDonald, & Francis, 2007; Bryant, 1990; Catts, 1986; DeJong, 2007; Stanovich, 1988; Wagner, Torgeson, & Rashotte, 1994). This may seem like a small feat, but agreement in the field of education can be compared with passing a local budget item through the school board that calls for a 25% increase in teachers' salaries for the next year. In other words, it is unheard of.

For years, the field of education has debated the merits of different reading approaches (whole word vs. phonics vs. whole language vs. literature-based vs. linguistics, etc.). The list goes on and on. The problem is that many of these approaches were widely distributed before research backed the results. It seems that reading instruction has had more fads than Paris has had hemlines. This poses a problem in the day and age of evidence-based decision making about instruction.

The difference here is that phonemic awareness—or the sensitivity to, or explicit awareness of, sound structure in words—is a key component to predicting reading success (Blachman, 1991; Pulakanaho et al., 2008; Torgesen, Morgan, & Davis, 1992; Wagner et al., 1994). Research has confirmed that less-skilled readers tend to have difficulty identifying, separating, and blending sound segments. In fact, research has shown that the apparent relationship between phonemic awareness and reading may be a causal one (Blachman, 1991; Torppa, Poikkeus, Laakso, Eklund, & Lyytinen, 2006). The relationship also appears to be independent of other abilities and even cognitive functioning (Anthony et al., 2007). Indeed, tests of phonemic awareness appear to do a better job predicting printed word recognition than do intelligence, language, or reading readiness measures. In addition, recent research has shown that phonemic awareness can be taught, and this instruction has positive influences on letter sound recognition and word recognition (Scott, 1995; Torgesen et al., 1992; Torppa et al., 2006). In a meta-analysis from the National Reading Panel convened by the U.S. Congress in 2000, scientific evidence was found to support the use of phonemic awareness instruction in learning to read. The panel found that phonological awareness instruction was more effective than alternative forms of instruction in helping children acquire reading and spelling skills (Ehri et al., 2001), Phonemic awareness is actually considered a prerequisite to learning to read by many professionals in the field of education. As Ehri (2005) states, the process of reading is "enabled by phonemic awareness and by knowledge of the alphabetic system" (p. 167).

■ DEFINITION

If phonemic awareness is to be considered a precursor to word recognition, it is important to adequately define the term *phonological awareness.* Phonological awareness is a special kind of sound knowledge. It is different than the phonological knowledge required in the comprehension or production of language. Phonological awareness requires a conscious alertness to the sound properties in speech. In other words, the focus of this language skill shifts from the content of speech to the form of speech. As children learn language, much time is spent on the development of language content. Children learn that candy is sweet, you eat it, you don't eat it at mealtime, Grandpa always has some with him, and the word *please* will almost always get you some. Phonemic awareness requires the child to know that the word *chocolate* has more sounds than the word *candy*, and that the two words begin with different sounds. Thus, phonological awareness can be defined as a person's sensitivity to or explicit knowledge of phonological or sound structures in the spoken words of a particular language. This awareness allows the individual to recognize and manipulate sound segments in spoken words (Anthony & Francis, 2005). It is sound awareness, not the ability to hear (acuity). It is the ability to understand speech at the sound level. Phonemic awareness is the specific ability to recognize and manipulate sounds at the phoneme, or individual sound level.

■ COMPLEXITY

Although you might think that this is a very simple task, it is very difficult for some children. Consider for a moment: do the words *cute* and *boot* rhyme? Does *cute* have a long *u* vowel? Does *boot* have the long *u* vowel sound? What's the difference in the long *u* vowel sound and the *oo* diphthong? Could the long vowel *u* actually be two sounds (/y/ and /oo/)? Children, particularly, have difficulty with the abstract nature of phonemic structure. To understand this complexity, try the following activities:

- Say the sound /b/ in isolation, without a vowel sound on the end.
- Think of the words *it* and *turtle*. Does the /t/ sound the same in each word? Look in the mirror. Does your mouth make the same shape for the /t/ in *it* and the /t/ in *turtle*?

As you have discovered, many sounds in our language, such as /p/ and /b/, do not exist in isolation, and often sounds change in relationship to the sounds that surround them.

PHONEMIC AWARENESS VERSUS PHONICS ■

You may still be unclear about the difference between phonemic awareness and phonics. This is a very confusing issue, because phonemic awareness is a part of the bigger construct of phonics. Phonics can be thought of as a union of three parts:

1. Phonemic awareness

2. Grapheme-phoneme, or letter-sound, correspondence

3. Structural analysis

Unfortunately, many instructional programs have focused so much on teaching letter-sound correspondence that often phonics has taken on that definition. To help understand phonemic awareness, here are some tips. Phonemic awareness is an auditory skill. Teaching letters or words is not a part of phonemic awareness instruction. Asking a child to tell which of two words is bigger, such as *dog* or *Dalmatian*, is presenting a phonemic awareness task. All of the games, activities, and lessons revolve around saying or identifying sounds from pictures. Grapheme-phoneme skills teach letter-sound agreement. Teaching a child that the word *bear* begins with the letter *b* is a grapheme-phoneme training technique. Structural analysis looks at word parts, such as prefixes, suffixes, compound words, etc. Unfortunately, educators have narrowed the focus of phonic instruction to the point that phonemic awareness and structural analysis are not always recognized as components of phonics and are thus left out.

RELATIONSHIP TO READING ■

All of us have worked with children who can produce the short *a* sound on command but are unable to read the word *crab* or they really don't hear a difference between the words *pen* and *pin*. The children who persist in sound task errors or who are unable to apply letter-sound knowledge beyond the normally accepted age are often the children with phonemic awareness deficits.

Characteristics of Children
With Phonemic Awareness Deficits

- Unable to hear the difference between sounds such as short /i/ and /e/
- Don't enjoy Dr. Seuss, because they just don't get it
- Can't do rhyming tasks
- Often mispronounce words by substituting sounds in words, such as pronouncing train as chrain (past the developmentally appropriate age)
- Can't blend isolated sounds to make words. They may say /c/ /a/ /t/ = "kit"

Research has examined young children's ability to perform on tests of phonemic awareness and later scores on tests of reading. Early research looked specifically at the correlation between phonemic awareness skills and later word recognition ability. During the 1970s, researchers found a strong positive correlation between what was then called auditory analysis, or phonemic analysis skills, and reading achievement scores at the end of first grade. Researchers found that future good readers possessed an awareness of abstract phonological relationships and that future poor readers rarely understood phonological structure. Perhaps the most important finding from these correlation studies was that many children at risk for reading failure could be reliably identified before the onset of reading instruction by the use of phonemic awareness tests (Catts, 1991; Stuart & Masterson, 1992). In a paper presented by Swank and Catts at the annual meeting of the International Reading Association in 1991, phonemic awareness was reportedly able to identify good readers with 85.7% accuracy and poor readers with 90.5% accuracy. The research on phonemic awareness, as related to early reading success, has been very conclusive. Children must acquire phonemic awareness skills before learning to read. Deficits in phonemic awareness skills often lead to an inability to make the connection between the spoken and written language and have been found to be a major contributor to reading disabilities such as those seen in remedial reading and learning disabilities programs (Ackerman & Dykman, 1993; Pulakanaho et al., 2008; Torppa, et al., 2006). Fortunately for most children, exposure to the alphabet automatically triggers phonemic awareness. However, some children lack phonemic awareness ability even after early literacy experiences. These are the children most often identified as having a reading disorder.

◼ TRAINING

Current research has focused on how phonemic awareness can be trained and if that training has an effect on beginning reading and reading disabilities. Research has concluded that phonemic awareness skills can be taught. They can be developed before reading instruction and independently of it (Bryne & Fielding-Barnsley, 1991). Studies clearly show that phonemic awareness is learnable at the preliterate stage in development and that systematic training of phonemic awareness abilities facilitates both reading and spelling acquisition. Additional studies have shown that the training also is successful with older children and even with children identified as having a disability (Scott, 1995). Possibly the most exciting result of these numerous studies is the transfer of phonemic awareness training to early reading skills. In fact, phonemic awareness training has been found to be a powerful new strategy for teaching children how to read words (Alexander, Andersen, Heilman, Voller, & Torgesen, 1991; Brennan & Ireson, 1997; Scott, 1995).

COMPONENTS   ■

The ability to recognize and manipulate sound segments is usually the focus of phonemic awareness training. Phonemic awareness skills can typically be separated into the following four different categories:

1. Phoneme identification and comparison

2. Phoneme segmentation

3. Phoneme blending

4. Rhyming

These categories reflect the most frequently used tasks researchers have devised to evaluate and train students on the knowledge of the sound structure in words. They are often used in combination with one another. In fact, a good training program will include all of the phonemic awareness components (Yopp, 1992). Exposure to several kinds of phonemic tasks provides a richer awareness and is more likely to generalize to reading acquisition. It is important to note that all of the following tasks require only the oral pronunciation or a picture to represent a word. This is the key to effective phonemic awareness instruction. Instruction that uses the written word is teaching something other than phonemic awareness.

PHONEME IDENTIFICATION AND COMPARISON   ■

The most common type of phonemic awareness instruction has historically been phoneme identification and comparison. A first-grade teacher might ask students, "Buffalo begins with what sound?" This is a type of phonemic awareness instruction. In phoneme identification, the student is frequently asked to say what sound is heard at the beginning, middle, or end of a particular word shown in picture form. Phoneme identification can be done in a matching or recall format. Matching tasks are easier than recall tasks, because they require only recognition of the correct answer instead of recall of something that isn't there. Matching tasks ask the subject to choose which words contain the same sound from a set of pictures. The child might either be given a picture or be presented with words orally. Then the child is asked to identify which word begins, ends, or has the same middle sound as the first one given. For example, the child will be shown a picture of a dog and a cat. The teacher would ask, "Which one starts with the same sound as donkey?"

Another form of this type of instruction asks students to recall a different word that begins or ends the same. Teachers may ask, "Tell me a word that begins with a /sh/ sound." I caution you to use this activity wisely, because "shoe" may be less likely to come out of the mouths of some little darlings than "sh#@**t." I learned this the hard way!

In phoneme comparison, students are asked to make decisions about two or more phonemes. That is, they are asked to identify commonalities and differences at the phoneme level in words. Phoneme oddity is one such task. Phoneme oddity tasks require the student to identify which one word in a group of words has a different sound. The teacher may ask which word begins differently, ends differently, or has a different middle sound. Typically, three pictures are presented, with the word for each picture. The child is then instructed to identify the word that does not belong to the category. For example, the student may be given pictures of a pig, a pen, and a tree. The teacher would ask, "Which one begins differently?" Or the task could focus on ending sounds. In this type of task, the child could be shown a house, a rabbit, and a dress. Then the student is asked to choose the picture of the one that ends with a different sound. Remember Sesame Street and "Which one of these things doesn't belong?"

■ PHONEME SEGMENTATION

Segmentation taps into the individual's ability to break apart the phonological structure within words. Children are asked to do a variety of tasks involving the separation of individual sounds or sound chunks in words. The most commonly taught segmentation skill is breaking words into syllables. Another chunking activity asks students to break words down into onset and rime. Onset is the first sound before the vowel, and rime is the vowel sound and the remaining part of the word. For example, *look* would be broken into the parts of /l/ and /ook/.

Another form of phoneme segmentation is deletion. Phoneme deletion requires children to separate the sounds in words and then pronounce the word while leaving out a particular sound. Students are asked to delete the first, middle, or last sound they hear and pronounce what is left. The word *farm* would become the word *arm* (initial deletion), *fm* (medial deletion), or *far* (final deletion).

Children also are often taught to separate words into the individual sounds. I have made a robot puppet and asked my students to "talk in robot language" by saying the individual sounds. Thus, the word *black* would be pronounced /b/ /l/ /a/ /k/.

The most complex segmentation task is counting phonemes. In a counting task, the individual is often given a word such as *cat* and asked to tell how many individual sounds are heard. The appropriate answer for this item would be three. This is often a foreign task for students and takes several instructional periods before the student masters the concept. Children commonly tell the number of letters in the word, showing a poor understanding of the sound/symbol relationship. It is best to begin with some sort of manipulative to help in the separation of the sounds. I have often asked students to take a dinosaur counter out of a basket for every sound they hear in a word or hold up a finger for every sound in a word.

Using such things as coins, bear counters, or buttons to aid short-term memory has been found to help with phoneme counting in beginning instruction. It also makes the task more active.

PHONEME BLENDING ■

Blending tasks require the subject to synthesize phonemes into words. Phonemes are commonly pronounced by the teacher in isolation, and the child is asked to blend the phonemes into a word. Therefore, /c/ /a/ /t/ would be blended into the word *cat*. Another task used to teach blending asks the student to choose the picture that corresponds with individual phonemes presented orally. For example, the student might be asked to choose the correct picture for the phonemes /d/ /u/ /k/.

RHYMING ■

Rhyming is a phoneme substitution task. Phoneme substitution involves changing a particular phoneme in a word to make a new word. Rhyming is a complex skill that requires identification, segmentation, and blending. The child is given a word such as gate and asked to say the word, but instead of using a /g/ sound in the beginning, put an /l/ sound in the beginning.

SUMMARY OF THE FACTS
ABOUT PHONEMIC AWARENESS ■

- Phonemic awareness is a special kind of sound knowledge.
- It shifts the emphasis from the content of speech to the form of speech.
- It is a very complex skill.
- It accounts for much of the variability in reading acquisition.
- It is a part of phonics.
- It is a key component in predicting reading success.
- It is a contributing factor in reading disabilities.
- It has four major components: identification and comparison, segmentation, blending, and rhyming.
- Phonemic awareness training has a positive effect on reading ability.
- This training is only one part of a balanced reading program.

2

Teaching and Assessing Phonemic Awareness

■ INSTRUCTION

Although phonemic awareness training is not a new instructional method, it has attained revitalization within the last 10 years. Recently, research has suggested that phonemic awareness training is most effective when incorporated into reading instruction (Hatcher, Hulme, & Ellis, 1994). In other words, phonemic awareness training should be a part of reading instruction and should be designed as an extension to authentic literacy tasks. As proposed by Adams and Henry, reading instruction must be built upon phonemic awareness, but it also should be complemented and reinforced though a variety of reading and writing activities (1997).

The terms phonological awareness and phonemic awareness are not interchangeable. Phonological awareness is the more global of the two terms and includes the ability to manipulate language into units such as words, syllables, and phonemes. Phonemic awareness is the subset of skills within phonological awareness that specifically refers to the manipulation of sound into the smallest unit of sound, or phoneme. Therefore, it becomes necessary to facilitate the development of phonological awareness skills before phonemic awareness. This is where implicit instruction with children's literature, finger plays, nursery rhymes, and songs is vitally important.

To capitalize on the strength of phonological awareness training, teachers must learn how to incorporate the phonemic awareness skills into existing reading instruction, with the ultimate focus on reading compre-hension. In fact, phonemic awareness should be taught by both implicit and explicit instruction. Phonemic awareness instruction should combine implicit instruction, such as reading literature that plays with sounds and singing songs that manipulate sounds, and explicit instruction that focuses on systematic and direct presentation of skills.

The key to phonological awareness training is the representation of words in auditory or picture format. A teacher who writes the words rabbit and elephant on the board and asks the students to divide the words into syllables is not necessarily working on phonological awareness. This task is more of a phonics task. For the teacher to make this task focus on phonological awareness, she should present the words orally or use a picture. As students progress in their phonological awareness skills, it is important to make the connection to letters. However, letters and decod-ing should be presented only after students have achieved some basic skills in phonological awareness. As students master phonological awareness skills, training should include information on phonemes and their corresponding letters. The addition of phonemic awareness and let-ter recognition has been found to have a better effect on a student's decoding and spelling abilities (Adams & Henry, 1997; Ball & Blachman, 1991; Manyak, 2008).

COMPONENTS OF EFFECTIVE INSTRUCTION ■

It is important to remember that before students actually practice a skill, they must be instructed on that skill. In the instructional phase, the teacher defines the skill being taught, explains how the skill is used, describes when to use the skill, and models the skill. This is essential in phonemic awareness training.

Modeling is often the key to phonemic awareness instruction because of the abstract nature of phonemic awareness for some students. In other words, the instruction and definition of the skill won't make any sense to students who can't think about language on a phonemic level (Snider, 1995). In the modeling stage, the teacher should "think aloud" by talking about what is going through his head when doing a phonemic awareness task. The teacher should emphasize mouth formations seen when particu-lar sounds are produced. For example, you smile when you make the sound associated with the long *e*. The teacher also should discuss where the tongue is within the mouth, and what key word, sound, or action is associated with the phoneme. For example, the short *o* sound is associ-ated with the sound you make when the doctor wants to look in your throat.

It also is important to remember that phonemic awareness instruction should be developmentally appropriate. Middle school students should not be engaged in rhyming finger plays regardless of the students' cogni-tive abilities. When designing phonemic awareness instruction for older students, it is important to use materials that look age appropriate. Instead of moving colored blocks to count sounds, they might draw small circles on a piece of paper to show the number of sounds heard in a word. It is essentially the same task; one is just more adult in its design.

■ LEVELS OF INSTRUCTION

Teachers must address the hierarchical levels of instruction when designing phonemic awareness tasks. By addressing the level of instruction, teachers build from the most basic to the most complex levels of learning. The six levels of instruction include the following:

1. Awareness

2. Recognition

3. Recall

4. Application

5. Maintenance

6. Generalization

At the awareness level, the student is given the opportunity to explore the existence of the skill. In other words, the student is led to a discovery. In the awareness level, the teacher begins to shift instruction from the content to the form of speech. The teacher talks about the nature of language. The teacher may discuss the number of individual words in a sentence by having students clap out words from a sentence presented orally. Additionally, the teacher may make students aware of certain sounds heard in words. Teachers can discuss words with many sounds, such as *veterinarian*, or words with only a few sounds, such as *bee*. Having the students decide which word is longer builds an awareness for the complexity of sounds in words. For older students, the teacher should point out that letters don't always determine the sounds in the words. For instance, the word *of* has a /v/ sound but contains the letter *f*. One of the best ways to get students to think about sounds in words is by playing the "I'm thinking" game. The teacher picks an item to describe. However, instead of using content descriptions such as "You eat it," the teacher describes the word using phonemic principles. For example: "It is a word with many sounds," "It begins with a /d/ sound," "It ends with a /n/ sound," and so on, until the student guesses the word *Dalmatian*. In the beginning, the teacher may have to give content clues until the student gets the hang of the game. Because this is the awareness stage, the teacher should model each answer.

The recognition stage allows the student to discriminate between similar items. The student is allowed to choose the correct answer from detractors. In this stage, it is important for the teacher to model or explain why or why not each answer is correct or incorrect. For example, the teacher might ask, "Which word rhymes with *can—cat* or *pan*?" allowing the student to choose the correct answer. Once the student chooses an answer, the teacher would slowly pronounce each word and model *why* pan is the correct choice and cat is incorrect. Recognition is a simpler task than recall but allows students to build skills without being given the answer.

In the recall level, the student is required to produce the answer. Students must rely on their own memory and inner resources to generate ideas to perform the task. For this skill, the teacher would simply say, "Tell me a word that rhymes with *can*."

Application requires students to use knowledge acquired earlier in new and meaningful ways. Often, application provides students with the opportunity to problem-solve with their knowledge. In the application level, the teacher might read a story and have students identify rhyming words in the story. The students would be asked to discuss why some rhyming books or poems have words that do not really rhyme. For example:

Down in the meadow where the grass grows even

Lived a mother jackrabbit and her little babies seven.

The language flows, but the words even and seven do not rhyme. Students at the application stage should be able to identify when words rhyme and when they do not in poetry.

In the maintenance and generalization level, the teacher's focus is getting students to retain and use information. Building accuracy, fluency, and automaticity is vital for maintenance. Through both drill/practice and application, students enhance their long-term memory for skill and, in turn, increase the likelihood they will be able to generalize information to new situations and various settings.

LEVELS OF PHONOLOGICAL AWARENESS ■

To assist the development of sound manipulation, teachers should consider the levels of complexity in phonological awareness tasks. The general rule of thumb is to teach larger units before smaller units. Teachers should begin by giving students sentences and asking them to identify the individual words in the sentences. Then, the teacher can progress to asking students to work at the word level by separating compound words, such as birdhouse, into separate words. Next, the teacher can move to the syllable level, where students blend syllables together to make a word or segment words into distinctive syllables. Although syllables are very abstract in nature, most children can identify syllables by clapping each syllable or by watching for your chin to drop as you say a word. Because each syllable has a vowel sound, the mouth falls open when saying each syllable. Instruct the students to hold their hands under their chins as they say the word. When their chins force their hands down, that is a syllable. At this point, students can be taught to identify *onset* and *rime*. *Onset* is the word's initial consonant or consonant combination. The *rime* is the remaining part of the word that begins with a vowel sound ("rime" is different from "rhyme" in that *rime* is a series of letters that are the same but don't always make the same sound, such as *ear* and *bear;* rhymes involve a series of letters that may be different but make the same sound). For example, in the word *chair, ch* is the onset and *air* is the rime. Once students have mastered the manipulation of larger units of sound, they are ready to begin manipulation at the phoneme, or individual sound, level (phonemic awareness). At this level, students blend, segment, delete, or otherwise manipulate individual sounds in words.

At each of the preceding levels, students should be instructed to identify and compare, segment, and blend. Students can identify or detect, segment, and/or blend:

1. Words in sentences

2. Words within compound words

3. Syllables

4. Onset and rime

5. Phonemes

Addition and deletion tasks also can be done at the sentence, word, syllable, onset/rime, and phoneme level. The teacher can begin these tasks at the sentence level by giving students a sentence such as "The brown bear ran" and asking them to add a word such as *big* to the sentence or delete a word such as *brown* from the sentence. At the phoneme level, students are given a word and asked to put a sound on the beginning or end of the word. If given the word *far* and asked to add the ending sound /m/, the word becomes *farm*. If given the word *rink* and asked to delete the beginning sound /r/, the word becomes *ink*. The addition of several beginning sounds naturally lends itself to rhyming. A task related to addition and deletion that is appropriate for older students is phoneme reversal in words. For instance, the teacher would say the word *teach* and ask students to reverse the order of phonemes in the word or to say the word backward. The student would then pronounce the word *cheat*.

Rhyming is a complex task requiring a level of abstraction. However, it is often easy for many children because it presents a familiar activity many parents and teachers do with preschool children. Rhyming is common in finger plays, songs, and many children's books designed for young children. Thus, rhyming may be a good place to begin the development of phonological awareness. For older students with phonological awareness deficits, writing poetry or raps that include rhyming words is a developmentally appropriate skill to facilitate rhyming skills.

Generally speaking, continuous sounds should be taught before stop sounds (Snider, 1995). Continuous sounds are those that can be stretched out. All vowel sounds are continuous. Stop sounds include /b/, /c/, /d/, /g/, /h/, /j/, /k/, /p/, /q/, and /x/. They are more difficult because they are difficult to say in isolation. Typically, a schwa vowel sound, the sound heard at the beginning of the word *about*, is inadvertently added to the end so /d/ becomes *duh*. This can cause confusion for students. Likewise, words with fewer sounds are easier to work with than words with more sounds. Initial and final blends also are difficult. Students tend to pronounce blends together such as /tr/ "ain" instead of /t/ /r/ "ain." Words containing the letter r can be difficult to explain and harder to deal with. For instance, how many sounds do you hear in the words *car* and *ear?* These sounds are better left out until the student has some basic understanding of phonological awareness.

For students experiencing difficulty perceiving the sounds in words, there are several simple, yet effective, devices that can be used to help auditory discrimination. Using a mirror to watch the way words and phonemes are pronounced allows students to have visual images for sounds. Also, a curved piece of PVC pipe (purchased at your local hardware store) held to the ear and mouth like a phone can magnify sound, allowing a student to detect subtle differences in phonemes.

Counting sounds or sound chunks, using manipulatives such as blocks, small candies, or beads on a string, or even drawing circles on a piece of paper to represent the sounds are nice ways to provide a visual representation for sounds. Teachers may want to introduce the concept of phonemic counting by asking children to count the number of words in a sentence that begin with a particular sound. It's always fun to use counters that start with the sound of study. For example, the teacher might want to use bear counters when identifying words that begin with a /b/ sound.

ASSESSMENT ■

Phonological awareness can be assessed in several different ways. An appropriate activity for young children is to give them two words, such as *car* and *butterfly*, and ask them to identify the word with more sounds or the bigger word. Children with weaker phonological awareness skills will picture a car and a butterfly and say "car" because a car is larger than a butterfly.

As students get older, they can be presented with a picture and asked to find another picture that begins with the same sound. The teacher would place three cards in front of the student. The cards would have pictures of a dog, a cat, and a horse. The teacher would then hold up a picture of a hammer and say, "Find the picture that begins with the same sound as the word *hammer*." The same activity can be done with ending sounds. The teacher would give the student the same three pictures and say, "Find the picture that ends with the same sound as *mouse*." It is best not to mix the two types of items. First, the students should be presented with tasks requiring initial identification. Then, students should be presented with tasks requiring final identification to avoid confusing the concepts "begin" and "end." Rhyming pairs can also be used. In this type of activity, the teacher would show a picture of a cat and ask the student to either "Find a picture that rhymes with cat" (a recognition task) or "Tell me a word that rhymes with cat" (a recall task). See the Resource for a progress chart for monitoring student development.

Reading and writing skills are intertwined. The use of invented spelling is an excellent tool to use with kindergarten and older children who can print. Invented spelling tasks can be used to identify phonemic awareness weaknesses and monitor student progress. Invented spelling is typical of children from preschool through early grades. Teachers can track the progress of a student's phonemic awareness through the progress of writing using five common patterns seen in invented spelling. These patterns include prephonemic, phonemic, letter name, traditional, and derivational spelling (Temple & Gillet, 1979). In the prephonemic spelling pattern, children write using letterlike forms in a horizontal row. In the second pattern, phonemic spelling, letters appear in short consonant strings. The third pattern is letter-name spelling. In this pattern, students use letters to represent sounds. The words are often spelled just as they are pronounced. It's common to see students spell *of* as *ov* and *cat* as *kat* during this pattern period. The transition pattern is typically used by students who have mastered basic phonemic awareness skills but aren't fluent yet. In this stage, letters are used to represent all sounds, or phonemes, and the student is using common spelling patterns for words with short vowels (C/V/V) and words with long vowels (C/V/V/e and C/V/V/C). In the fifth pattern, derivational spelling, students are beginning to use rule-governed conventions that are more sophisticated, such as consonant doubling. Tracking students in their progression of invented spelling can provide valuable insight into their phonemic awareness ability.

■ CONCLUSION

I was able to study the effect of phonemic awareness instruction on children in third grade who were experiencing difficulty with reading. Some of the children had identified reading disabilities and some did not. After only six weeks of training lasting 15 minutes a day, I was able to report that statistically significant differences existed in pre- and posttesting on measures of decoding and word recognition. From this study, I concluded that phonemic awareness training is a powerful tool in the remediation of reading disabilities. Thus, the addition of phonemic awareness instruction has been proven to produce dramatic effects on both (1) beginning reading acquisition for those with and without disabilities and (2) remediation of identified reading disabilities.

My work has shown this training to be very simple to implement. It is not meant to be a stand-alone reading program. Good reading instruction should focus on a balance between skill instruction and comprehension. Reading for meaning and comprehension skills such as sequencing, main idea, cause and effect, and predicting outcomes should be integral to every lesson. Phonemic awareness instruction should be embedded into good reading instruction and should not be an isolated skill. I have found success when using authentic children's literature, such as *Alexander and the Terrible, Horrible, No Good, Very Bad Day* by Judith Viorst. I like to choose pictures and words for the phonemic awareness instruction from the literature book we are using. I have found this technique to generalize better to decoding skills and, in turn, reading comprehension. I hope you will find the following lesson plans, games, and activities helpful in developing your own phonemic awareness instruction.

3
Collection of Lessons

Lessons

Lesson 1

Recognizing Phonemes in Words

OBJECTIVE: Students will be able to recognize that some words have more phonemes than other words. The focus shifts from the content to the form of speech.

MATERIALS: crayons, a clock with a second hand, and Activity Page D-1

■ REVIEW

"Who can tell me what words are made of?"

■ PREVIEW

"Today we are going to learn how sounds make words."

■ PRESENTATION/INSTRUCTION

"Words are made up of little parts called sounds. Some words have many sounds in them, and some words have only a few sounds in them. For now, don't think about the letters in words. Listen to the sound /ch/. Who knows how to spell that? Yes, it is spelled *ch*. How many sounds do you hear in /ch/? Only one! For /ch/, it takes two letters to make one sound. What sound does the letter *x* make? How many sounds do you hear? The letter *x* makes two sounds. You hear a /k/ and a /s/. Listen /b/ /o/ /k/ /s/ (box). Do you hear the /k/ and the /s/ sounds? Letters are tricky, so think about only the sounds. Sound listening is important, because it will help you learn to read or to be a better reader."

Model

"Let's listen to some words and see which one has more sounds."

car—grasshopper

"Let me think. A car, of course, is much bigger than a grasshopper. But we are listening to the words, not thinking about what the words mean.

(Say the words again slowly.) If I look at the clock, I can see that the second hand only moves a little when I say 'car' and moves more when I say 'grasshopper.' Everyone look at the clock with me. Let's say 'car.' How many seconds did that word take? Let's say 'grasshopper.' How many seconds did that word take? Even if I say 'grasshopper' really fast, it still takes longer to say than 'car.' It must have more sounds. Do you agree? To get this right, you have to think about the sounds in the words, not the meanings.

"The tricky thing about this is that sometimes the letters in a word don't tell us about the number of sounds in a word. Think about the word *are*. Does anyone know how to spell *are*? *(Write* are *on the board.)* How many letters are in the word *are*? Three is correct. How many sounds do you hear? Everyone put up a finger for the number of sounds you hear. If you had only one finger up, you were right. Great listening! The word *are* has only one sound." *(Depending on dialect,* are *may have two sounds: short /o/ and* /r/.) "This is the reason why it is important to learn to listen to sounds in words instead of thinking about what they mean or how they are spelled."

GUIDED PRACTICE   ■

"Now that we have learned how to listen to sounds in words, let's practice. I will say two words. Then I will count to three. When I say 'ready,' everyone will tell the word with the most sounds. So if I say 'caterpillar, toy,' what word would you say? Ready . . . yes, you would say 'caterpillar.'

"Let's do some more:"

lighting—key	Ready . . .
elephant—cat	Ready . . .
hippopotamus—bird	Ready . . .
dog—buffalo	Ready . . .
dragon—sit	Ready . . .
you—umbrella	Ready . . .

INDEPENDENT PRACTICE   ■

"Now I would like you to do the activity page and color the picture in each row that has the most sounds in its name. Remember do not think about the meaning of the word or the letters in the word, because that can trick you."

Activity Page D-1 Key

cap	cup	<u>pineapple</u>
hook	<u>volcano</u>	bat
top	jet	<u>pencil</u>
fish	cat	<u>dinosaur</u>

■ REVIEW

(Check activity page together when they are finished.)
"Today we learned that some words have more sounds than others. Who can tell me the two things that can trick you?"

- You have to think about the word sounds, not the meaning.
- You can't use the number of letters, because that doesn't always work.

■ PREVIEW

"Tomorrow we will work more with sounds."

Name _____

Color the picture in each row that has the most sounds.

Activity Page D-1

Lesson 2

Recognizing More Phonemes in Words

OBJECTIVE: Students will be able to recognize that some words have more phonemes than other words. The focus shifts from the content to the form of speech.

MATERIALS: pencil and paper

■ REVIEW

"Who can tell me what we did yesterday?"

■ PREVIEW

"Today we are going to learn more about sounds in words."

■ PRESENTATION/INSTRUCTION

"Remember yesterday we colored pictures that had the most sounds in their names? We found out that words are made of sounds and that some words have a lot of sounds and some words have only a few sounds.
    "Who can remember the two things that can trick you?"

- You have to think about the word sound, not the meaning.
- You can't use the number of letters, because that doesn't always work.

■ GUIDED PRACTICE

"Let's practice finding the longer word using our names. I have a friend named Beth, but her real name is Elizabeth. Which name is longer? How many of you have a nickname? Is your nickname longer or shorter than your full name?" *(Choose individual students to give their full names and nicknames, and let the class help decide which is longer.)* "Now let's find out if your name is longer or shorter than someone else's in the class." *(Choose two students to come to the front of the room and say their first names. Let the*

20

class decide who has the longer name. Try to choose pairs with marked differences in their names. Repeat this until everyone has had a chance.)

INDEPENDENT PRACTICE ■

"Now let's play a guessing game. I'm going to say a word, and you think of another word that goes with the word that I said—but your word must have more sounds than my word. If I said *tree*, you would tell me a kind of tree that has more sounds than the word *tree*. Would *oak* be right? No. Would *sycamore*? Yes! I'm going to divide the class into teams. The team that guesses a correct word first gets two points. The team with the most points at the end of the game wins." *(Stop taking guesses when the correct word has been identified, and give out points. Let the team guess only once after a clue is given. After one guess, they must wait until the next clue is given to guess again. If a guess is correct—e.g., large dog: collie—but not the one you're thinking of, say, "Good guess. It's correct but not the one I'm thinking of. Here is another clue.")*

- I'm thinking of a kind of dog. It has more sounds than the word *dog*. *(Take guesses.)*
- It's a large dog. *(Take guesses.)*
- There is a movie about it. *(Take guesses.)*
- This dog is black and white. *(Take guesses.)*
- It is white with black spots. *(Take guesses.)*
- The movie is called 101 . . . *(Take guesses.)*
- The word starts with a /d/ sound. *(Take guesses.)*

DALMATIAN

- I'm thinking of something that lives in the sea. It has more sounds than the word *sea. (Take guesses.)*
- It isn't a fish. *(Take guesses.)*
- It has a soft body. *(Take guesses.)*
- It has eight legs, or tentacles. *(Take guesses.)*
- The word starts with an /o/ sound. *(Take guesses.)*

OCTOPUS

- I'm thinking of a kind of bird. It has more sounds than the word *bird*. *(Take guesses.)*
- It's a small bird. *(Take guesses.)*
- It can fly very fast. *(Take guesses.)*
- It drinks nectar from flowers. *(Take guesses.)*
- The word starts with a /h/ sound. *(Take guesses.)*

HUMMINGBIRD

- I'm thinking of a kind of food. It has more sounds than the word *food. (Take guesses.)*
- It's a fruit. *(Take guesses.)*
- Some people eat them for breakfast. *(Take guesses.)*
- They grow in bunches. *(Take guesses.)*

- They are yellow. *(Take guesses.)*
- You peel them. *(Take guesses.)*
- Monkeys like to eat them. *(Take guesses.)*
- The word starts with a /b/ sound. *(Take guesses.)*

BANANA

- I'm thinking of a kind of day. It has more sounds than the word *day*. *(Take guesses.)*
- It's a holiday. *(Take guesses.)*
- We don't go to school on that day. *(Take guesses.)*
- It comes in the fall. *(Take guesses.)*
- A lot of us have a big meal with our families. *(Take guesses.)*
- We usually eat turkey. *(Take guesses.)*
- The word starts with a /th/ sound. *(Take guesses.)*

THANKSGIVING

- I'm thinking of a kind of bug. It has more sounds than the word *bug*. *(Take guesses.)*
- It's small and jumps. *(Take guesses.)*
- It can be brown, black, or green. *(Take guesses.)*
- It is considered good luck by the Chinese. *(Take guesses.)*
- It makes a chirping sound by rubbing its legs together. *(Take guesses.)*
- The word starts with a /cr/ sound. *(Take guesses.)*

CRICKET

- I'm thinking of a game. It has more sounds than the word *game*. *(Take guesses.)*
- It uses a ball. *(Take guesses.)*
- The ball does not bounce. *(Take guesses.)*
- You must wear special shoes. *(Take guesses.)*
- You roll the ball. *(Take guesses.)*
- It hits pins. *(Take guesses.)*
- A strike is when you knock all of the pins down. *(Take guesses.)*
- The word starts with a /b/ sound. *(Take guesses.)*

BOWLING

- I'm thinking of a kind of candy. It has more sounds than the word *candy*. *(Take guesses.)*
- It's hard. *(Take guesses.)*
- It doesn't melt in your hand. *(Take guesses.)*
- It often comes in sticks. *(Take guesses.)*
- Most of the time it is red and white. *(Take guesses.)*
- The word starts with a /p/ sound. *(Take guesses.)*

PEPPERMINT

(Add up the points and announce the winning team.)

"Now, I want you all to write one riddle like the ones just given, with three clues to your riddle. Also write the answer to your riddle."

For an enrichment activity or for older students, you could play a relay game. Divide the class into two teams. They line up at the front of the room. The students at the front of the line answer the question, and then move to the back of the line. You will give a word, and they must give a word that has more sounds and is related to the word you just gave. The first correct answer gets two points. If the other team has an equally acceptable word, they get one point. For example, you say "dog." The first student on Team One says "Poodle" first for two points. Then Team Two gets a chance, and the student says "Dalmatian" for one point. Those two players move to the back, and two more players have a chance to answer the question. Alternate which team gets to answer first.

Relay words. *(Have the other team decide if the word really does have more sounds than your word before you give points. You can go through the list more than once and have students come up with new words for each category.)*

car	city	fish	toy	candy	fruit
dog	bug	sport	cat	state	tree
hat	game	bird	job	bear	flower

(Add to the list from your science, social studies, or reading content.)

REVIEW ■

"Today we worked more on sounds in words."

PREVIEW

■

"Tomorrow we will learn more about sounds and how to listen for them in reading."

Lesson 3

Identification /d/

OBJECTIVE: *Students will be able to identify the /d/ phoneme at the beginning of words.*

MATERIALS: *pencil, paper, and stickers*

■ REVIEW

"Who can tell me what we have been working on with sounds in words?" *(Give appropriate feedback, and review any previously mastered content.)*

■ PREVIEW

"Today we are going to talk about the sound that starts the words *dragon, duck,* and *dog.* Does any one know what sound that is?"

■ PRESENTATION/INSTRUCTION

"Let's say the /d/ sound together. Look at my mouth while I make the /d/ sound. How did it look? My lips were apart a little but not a lot. My teeth also were apart. What else did you notice? My lips made a small flat oval. Good! Your tongue will tap behind your top teeth. Now turn to a neighbor and make the /d/ sound. Make sure your lips look like mine. Dandy! That word starts with a /d/ sound. Do you think you can pick out more /d/ sounds? If you need help, look at my mouth for the /d/ shape."

■ GUIDED PRACTICE

"Let's listen to some words to see if you can hear the /d/ sound in the beginning of the word. Every time I say a word that begins with the /d/ sound, you bark like a DOG. Ready?"

dollar   mitten   duck   dragon   baby   dinosaur

■ INDEPENDENT PRACTICE

"Now I'll read a story. I want you to use your pencil to make a mark on your paper every time you hear a word that begins with the /d/ sound.

(Students will make a tally mark for each word they hear that begins with a /d/ sound.) After we are done, I'll ask you how many marks you made, and we will see who can get the correct number. I will read the story slowly. Ready?"

Darin Dinosaur

<u>Darin</u> was a <u>dancing</u> <u>dinosaur</u>. He loved to <u>dart</u> and <u>dip</u> on the <u>dance</u> floor. He would <u>descend</u> <u>down</u> the stairs <u>dressed</u> in <u>diamonds</u>. But <u>Darin</u> had a <u>dilemma</u>. His <u>dance</u> <u>director</u> <u>declared</u> that his tail <u>dragged</u> out too far to <u>dance</u> at the <u>disco</u>. "Oh <u>dear</u>!" said his best friend, <u>Darla</u> <u>Duck</u>. "<u>Don't</u> <u>dismay</u>, my <u>dear</u>, we'll have the <u>disco</u> in the <u>dome</u> and <u>dance</u> till <u>dawn</u>!" "Oh <u>Darla</u>, you're a <u>doll</u>," said <u>Darin</u>. The <u>disco</u> was <u>delightful</u>, and <u>Darin</u> <u>danced</u> until the <u>donkeys</u> came home.

"How many words did you count that began with a /d/? Put your number on the top of your paper and circle it." *(Now go through the story slowly and make a mark on the chalkboard for each /d/ sound. Count the marks and reward the correct answers with stickers or put their names on the board as Dandy /d/ Detectives!)*

REVIEW ■

"Today we learned to listen for the /d/ sound and how our mouth moves to make a /d/. Let's make the /d/ sound. Turn to your neighbor and have them check your mouth position. Dynamite!"

PREVIEW ■

"Tomorrow we will work with more /d/ sounds."

Lesson 4

Deletion /d/

OBJECTIVE: Students will delete the initial /d/ sound on words to make new words.

MATERIALS: pencil and Activity Page D-2

■ REVIEW

"Who can tell me what we have been working on with sounds in words?" *(Give appropriate feedback, and review any previously mastered content.)*

■ PREVIEW

"We are going to continue working on the /d/ sound today."

■ PRESENTATION/INSTRUCTION

"Yesterday we learned that the /d/ sound makes the tongue tap the top of your mouth just behind your teeth. I'd like everyone to make the /d/ sound while I check to see if your mouth position is correct. *(Give individual feedback and correction.)* Great! Now let's say some /d/ words and stretch out the /d/ sound at the beginning of each word. Then we will take the /d/ sound off and see what word is left. Listen carefully as I show you how. The first word is *dare*. /d/ . . . *are*. Now if I take off the /d/ from /d/ . . . *air*, I have the word *air* left. Does everyone see how I did that? Let's try one together."

■ GUIDED PRACTICE

"The word is *drug*. Let's stretch out the /d/. *Drrrrug*. Let's say the sounds together, /d/ /r/ /u/ /g/. Now let's pause after the /d/ sound: /d/ . . . *rug*. What word is left? Everyone? Yes, the word *rug* is left. *(Use the same procedure for the following words.)*

     dear—ear   door—or

"Hey, let's try to speak in code. If I said, 'Don't drink diet dew,' what would you say if you took all of the /d/ sounds off the words? *Don't* would be ... *ont, drink* would be ... *rink, diet* would be ... *iet,* and *dew* would be ... *ew.* The sentence would be 'Ont rink iet ew.' Now you give your neighbor the code for the sentence, 'Dolls don't do dances.'"

INDEPENDENT PRACTICE   ■

"I'm going to pass out an activity page. You need to take the /d/ sound off the pictures in the first column and match them to the new word in the second column. If the first picture represented the word *deaf,* what picture would you be looking for in the second column? That's right—a letter *f.* Before you start, let's make sure you know what the pictures are in the first column. Put your finger on the picture as I say it: dart, deer, date, doe, deal, drip."

REVIEW   ■

"Today we worked on taking off the /d/ sound in words to make new words. Dandy deletion!"

PREVIEW   ■

"Tomorrow we will work with a new sound."

Name  _____

Say the name of the picture in the first column, then take off the /d/ sound. Draw a line to the picture of the new word you made.

Lesson 5

Identification /s/

OBJECTIVE: *Students will be able to identify the /s/ phoneme at the beginning and end of words.*

MATERIALS: *pencil, crayons, and Activity Page S-1*

REVIEW ■

"Who can tell me what we have been working on with sounds in words?" *(Give appropriate feedback, and review previously mastered content.)*

PREVIEW ■

"Today we are going to talk about the sound /s/ at the beginning and end of words."

PRESENTATION/INSTRUCTION ■

"Let's say the /s/ sound together. Look at my mouth while I make the /s/ sound. Was my mouth in the right position? My lips were apart a little but not a lot. My teeth were very close together, almost touching, and my lips were flat like a line. Now turn to a neighbor and make the /s/ sound. Make sure your lips look like mine. Yes! That word ends with an /s/ sound. Do you think you can pick out /s/ sounds at the end of words?"

GUIDED PRACTICE ■

"I am going to say some words that have the /s/ sound in them. We are going to be listening for words that start with the /s/ sound. Everyone use thumbs up or thumbs down to tell me if these words start with the /s/ sound. Remember to watch my mouth."

straw   cats   sign   stink   soda   octopus

"Now, I am going to read you a story that has many /s/ sounds in it. We are going to be listening for words that end with the /s/ sound. First, let's practice. Everyone use thumbs up or thumbs down to tell me if these words end with the /s/ sound. Remember to watch my mouth."

dance   sack   vase   goose   last   bus

29

■ INDEPENDENT PRACTICE

"Now I'll read the story. I want you to hold your hand up every time you hear a word that ends with the /s/ sound. I will read the story slowly. Ready?"

<u>Once</u> there was a <u>mouse</u> that lived in a <u>house</u> that was a <u>mess</u>. There were things all over the <u>place</u>!

"Some of the things end with an /s/ sound. Listen and raise your hand for each thing ending with the /s/ sound."

<u>rice</u>	<u>socks</u>	<u>rocks</u>	<u>glass</u>	dirt	<u>books</u>
brush	<u>ice</u>	<u>shirts</u>	<u>lace</u>	soap	dish
<u>lice</u>	cash	<u>purse</u>	<u>box</u>	string	<u>cats</u>

"Let's draw a picture of that house." (*Pass out house activity page.*) "What things will you put in it? Remember to put in things that end with the /s/ sound. Do not write the words. Use pictures to represent the words that end with /s/."

■ REVIEW

"Today we learned to listen for the /s/ sound at the end of words. Let's make the /s/ sound. Turn to your neighbor and have them check your mouth position. Yesssss, yesssss, yesssss!!"

■ PREVIEW

"Tomorrow we will work more with /s/ sounds."

Name _____

Activity Page S-1

Lesson 6

Identification and Segmentation /s/

OBJECTIVE: Students will demonstrate the ability to isolate initial and final phonemes in words by pronouncing the /s/ phoneme in an exaggerated way such as "sssssssss . . . ound" or "bu . . . sssssssss."

MATERIALS: popsicle sticks, scissors, and Activity Pages S-2 and S-3 (copied onto tagboard)

■ REVIEW

"Who can tell me what sound we have been working on and what we have learned to do?" *(Give appropriate feedback.)* "Before we start, let's practice making the /s/ and check your neighbor's mouth position to make sure it is correct." *(Review any other previously mastered content.)*

■ PREVIEW

"Today we are going to pick out the /s/ sound in words that either begin or end with that sound."

■ PRESENTATION/INSTRUCTION

"Let's start by having you tell me words that you remember from our other lesson that begin with the /s/ sound." *(After the student says the word, the teacher repeats the word, holding out the /s/ sound such as sssss . . . ick. Make sure to pronounce words with blends by separating the consonants. For example, star would be pronounced "sssssssss . . . tar," exaggerating the /t/ sound.)* "Everyone say the word after me, and stress the /s/ sound as I do. Now, who can give me some words that end with a /s/ sound?" *(Again pronounce the words by isolating and holding out the /s/ sound as in "bu . . . sssss.")* When I am finished saying the word, I want you to say it just as I did.

"You are all getting so good at finding the /s/ sound. I have a picture of a ssss . . . nake head and a ssss . . . nake tail for each of you. I want you to color the two pictures, cut them out, and glue each one to a popsicle stick." *(Use Activity Page S-2. To save time, you may want to have this done for the class.)* "When you are done, we are going to do an activity."

GUIDED PRACTICE ■

"Now that everyone has a snake head and tail, I'm going to say some words with the /s/ sound in them. If the word *starts* with the /s/ sound, I want you to hold up the snake *head* and say the word by stressing the /s/ sound, as I just showed you. If the word *ends* with the /s/ sound, hold up the snake tail and say the word, stressing the /s/ sound. I want to hear a lot of /s/ sounds." *(I like to use my snake puppet for this activity.)* "Let's do the first few together." *(Practice as a group with these words.)*

bass	sack	seven	dress	sun	saw
place	seal	goose	mouse	chase	six

INDEPENDENT PRACTICE ■

"First, I am going to put you into groups of two. Then, I am going to give each group two sets of pictures. Cut the pictures apart to make cards. You will put the cards facedown in the center and take turns drawing a card. To keep the card, you have to say the /s/ word and tell if the word begins or ends with the /s/ sound. If I held up this card *(hold up a picture of a fish)* and you said 'fish,' would that be right? NO, because fish doesn't begin or end with the /s/ sound. What word would be correct? Yes, *ba . . . sss.*" *(Encourage several answers to show that there is more than one correct answer.)* "You must stress the /s/, like me . . . ssss or sssss . . . ap. If you say it correctly, you keep the card. If you don't get it correct, the card is turned back over and another player can have a chance to choose that picture. When all the cards are gone, the game is over.

"I want you to all be sssssuper sssssounders!"

The two Activity Pages for S-3 should be copied onto tagboard. Make one set (of the two pages) for each pair of students to use.

Activity Page S-3 Picture Key:

Initial /s/ page:

socks	sink	sack
soap	saw	sun
snake	sandwich	seal
snail	strawberry	splash

Final /s/ page:

nurse	dice	house
mouse	vase	box
face	fox	bass
dress	goose	bus

Game card variations: (1) For older students, you may want to use the cards to play a memory game and match two cards that begin with the /s/ sound or end with the /s/ sound. (2) Students also could play a game of Sound War. First, shuffle the cards and put them in the center of the table. Each student takes a turn flipping the card over. The students must say "beginning" or "end" (depending on where the /s/ sound is heard). The first one to identify the position of the /s/ gets to keep the card. The student with the most cards at the end of the game wins.

■ REVIEW

"I want everyone to think of a word that begins or ends with the /s/ sound. When I call your name, say your word, stressing the /s/ sound."

■ PREVIEW

"Tomorrow we will begin work on a new sound."

Activity Page S-2

Glue here.

Glue here.

Activity Page S-3b

Lesson 7

Deletion /a/ /s/

OBJECTIVE: Students will be able to delete the initial /a/ or /s/ sound in words to form a new word.

MATERIALS: two stuffed animals or sock puppets, scissors, and Activity Page A-1

■ REVIEW

"Who can tell me what we have been working on with sounds in words?" (Give appropriate feedback, and review any previously mastered content.)

■ PREVIEW

"Today we are going to work on the /a/ sound. Who knows what letter makes the /a/ sound? That's correct; it is the letter *a*."

■ PRESENTATION/INSTRUCTION

"Today, I am going to introduce you to a couple of my friends. They are Abbey and Adar." (*I have made sock puppets or used stuffed animals to represent Abbey and Adar.*) "Both of their names start with the /a/ sound. Watch my mouth as I slowly pronounce their names." (*Stress the short /a/ sound as you pronounce the names.*) "Let's all make the /a/ sound. Look at your neighbor's mouth. Did it make the same shape as mine?

"Watch my mouth as I read a story. Use your pencil to make a mark every time you hear a word that begins with the /a/ sound."

Abbey and Adar

Abbey and Adar are animals. On cool afternoons, they eat apples. "These are no average apples," said Adar. "May I have another?" "Absolutely," replied Abbey. Abbey is an athlete, and Adar is great at addition. It is time for Adar to go, but they will eat apples another day.

"How many words did you count that began with an /a/? Put your number on the top of your paper and circle it." (*Now go through the story slowly, and make a mark on the chalkboard for each /a/ sound. Count the marks, and reward the correct answers with stickers or put their names on the board as STAR SOUNDERS!*)

"Who was this story about? Everyone say 'Abbey and Adar' together. If I say 'Abbey' and stretch out the /a/ sound, I can pick out another word inside of the word Abbey." *(Stress the short /a/ sound as you pronounce the name: Aaaa . . . bee.)* "Can you find a little word inside the word *Abbey*? Yes, if you took off the /a/ sound, the word *bee* would be left. What about *Adar*? Is there a small word inside the word *Adar*? Thumbs up if you hear a small word; thumbs down if the leftover sounds do not make a real word. If you have your thumb down, you are correct. *Dar* is not a word."

GUIDED PRACTICE ■

"Let's try to find some more words by taking off the /a/ sound at the beginning of the words I will say." *(Pronounce each word slowly, stress the /a/ sound, and isolate the remaining sounds in the word. I like to put my hands up above my head for the /a/ sound and let them drop when I pronounce the remaining part of the word.)*

| <u>Abbey</u> | animal | ask | ashes | add |
| ant | Adar | <u>apple</u> | axe | after |

"How many of those words had a smaller word left when we took off the /a/ sound? Not many. *Abbey* had the word *bee* and *apple* had the word *pull.*

"We have also worked with the /s/ sound. Let's try to take off the beginning /s/ sound and find any smaller words." *(Pronounce each word slowly, stress the /s/ sound, and isolate the remaining sounds in the word. Then call on individuals to identify the remaining sound. Have the students do thumbs up if the sounds form a word and thumbs down if they do not.)*

<u>sad</u>   sack   <u>sat</u>   sap   <u>sink</u>
<u>sold</u>

"Good, you found four words: *add, at, ink,* and *old.*"

INDEPENDENT PRACTICE ■

"Now, let's play a Sound-O game." *(It is like bingo, except you need only three in a row to win.)* "I am going to give you a sheet of paper with pictures. Cut up

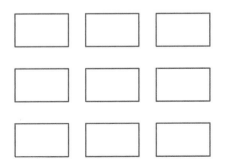

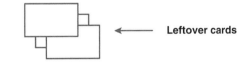

← **Leftover cards**

the pictures and place nine of them in front of you in three rows of three. You will have leftover cards. Stack them and put them on the corner of your desk."

Write these words on cards and shuffle them to call out:

soak	apple	sink	address
sea	Abbey	seal	snail
so	socks	slip	allege

"When I call out a word, you must take off the beginning sound, find the picture of the remaining word, and turn it over. When you get three in a row—across, up and down, or diagonally—yell out 'SOUND-O!' You must then say the words back with either the /s/ or the /a/ on the beginning, so I can check your three in a row." (*You can also play four corners, checkerboard, or black-out bingo.*) "Now let's go over the pictures on the sheet I am passing out. Put your finger on the picture as I say it."

Pictures: (*Go over all the pictures with the students before they cut them up.*)

oak	pull	ink	dress
E	bee	eel	nail
O	ox	lip	ledge

"So, if I said *sea*, what picture would you turn over? Yes, the *E*, because if you take the /s/ off of *sea*, *E* is what you would hear. Do you all understand how to play?"

■ REVIEW

"Who can tell me what we learned today? What two sounds did we work with? Remember how your mouth formed to make the /a/ sound? I want everyone to think of a word in which you found a little word inside." (*Call on an individual to tell their word and demonstrate taking off the initial sound.*) "Great work!"

■ PREVIEW

"Tomorrow we will continue working with the /a/ sound."

Lesson 8

Identification /a/

OBJECTIVE: *Students will be able to identify the /a/ sound when heard in both the initial and medial positions in words.*

MATERIALS: *Activity Pages A-2 (one set per group of two to four players) run off on tagboard and cut apart*

■ REVIEW

"Who can tell me what we have been working on with sounds in words?" *(Give appropriate feedback, and review any previously mastered content. Demonstrate mouth position for the /a/ sound.)*

■ PREVIEW

"For the past couple of days, we have been working on the /a/ sound. Today we are going to play a game."

■ PRESENTATION/INSTRUCTION

"First we worked on words that began with the /a/ sound. Who can tell me some words that begin with /a/? Then we worked on words that had an /a/ sound in the middle. Who can tell me some words with the /a/ in the middle?"

■ GUIDED PRACTICE

"Let's see how fast you can be at identifying the /a/ sound. I'll say two words. Only one is an /a/ word. The /a/ sound can come either at the beginning or middle of the word. After I say the words, I'll say 'ready,' and you all call out the /a/ word. Let's try to go fast."

(Call out the word pairs and then say "ready." Get progressively faster.)

ape	<u>add</u>	*Ready . . .*	<u>address</u>	late	*Ready . . .*
sailor	<u>sack</u>	*Ready . . .*	<u>ax</u>	soap	*Ready . . .*
<u>lap</u>	lot	*Ready . . .*	lemon	<u>last</u>	*Ready . . .*
<u>sap</u>	sit	*Ready . . .*	athlete	airplane	*Ready . . .*

INDEPENDENT PRACTICE   ■

(Divide the students into groups of two to four players.) "We are going to play a game. It is called Slap /a/. Have you ever played Slap Jack? It is like Slap Jack, only you will slap the picture of the /a/ word. Each group will get a deck of picture cards. Sit in a circle, and put the cards in the center, facedown. You will take turns flipping the cards and putting the new card on the flipped pile. When an /a/ picture comes up, the first one to slap the card gets to keep it and all the cards under it. Remember the /a/ sound can come at the beginning or middle of the word, so think carefully. If you slap a picture of a word that isn't an /a/ word, you lose two cards from your pile. If you slap someone's hand hard, you lose three cards—so play gently. The player with the most cards when all the cards are gone is the Absolute /a/ Master."

Activity Page A-2 Picture Key

(Go over the picture names before you play the game to avoid confusion.)

ashes	ax	apple
address	add	ant
alligator	anchor	astronaut
soap	can	cat
purse	ham	bag
paw	fox	peacock
fence	bee	bass
socks	goose	bat
pencil	jet	top
pillow	pen	nurse
sink	ox	rain
mouse	balloons	chick

To make the game more challenging, the students might have "slap" words with both the /a/ and the /s/ sound in them.

REVIEW   ■

"Tell me some /a/ words you learned today. Tell me some words that aren't /a/ words. All the Absolute /a/ Masters stand up and take a bow."

PREVIEW   ■

"Tomorrow, we are going to work with the /a/ sound again."

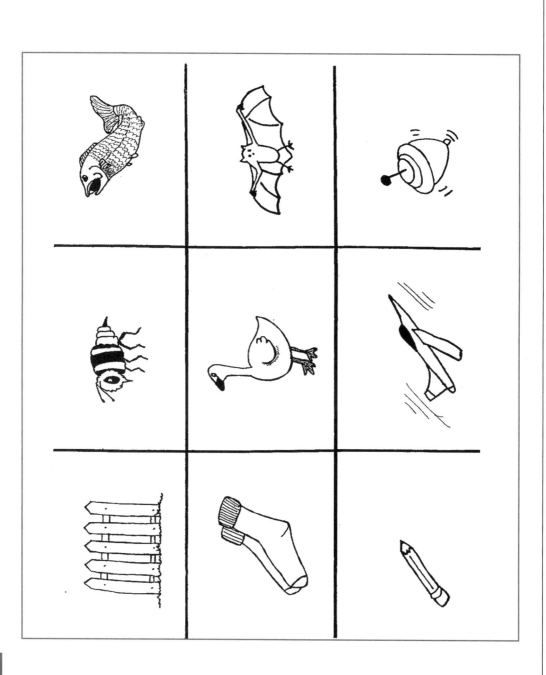

Activity Page A-2c

Lesson 9

Blending /a/

OBJECTIVE: *Students will blend three sounds, including a medial short /a/ to make new words.*

MATERIALS: *pencils and Activity Page A-3*

■ REVIEW

"Who can tell me what we have been working on with sounds in words? What sounds have we worked on? Who remembers what vowel we were working on yesterday? Yes, the /a/." *(Give appropriate feedback, and review any previously mastered content.)*

■ PREVIEW

"Today we are going to work with some words that have an /a/ in the middle of them."

■ PRESENTATION/INSTRUCTION

"I know that *apple* and *Abbey* start with an /a/ sound. What other words start with an /a/ sound? Everyone think of a word that begins with an /a/ and turn to your neighbor and share your word. Did your neighbor's mouth form the same position? Look carefully to make sure you know what an /a/ mouth looks like, because I'm going to try to trick you."

■ GUIDED PRACTICE

"Watch my mouth and listen carefully as I say some words. Put your thumb up if you hear an /a/ in the middle of the word. Put your thumb down if you do not hear an /a/ in the middle."
   (Say these words slowly and wait for the students' responses. After each word, put your thumb up or down to correct errors. Talk about how car *is spelled with an* a *but you do not hear /a/ in the word.)*

<u>cat</u>	car	gate	apple	star	<u>bag</u>
<u>sad</u>	hot	cup	jar	<u>fan</u>	laugh

"Now let's try to make some /a/ words. I want three people to come up here and stand in front of the class." *(Pick three students.)* "I will say a word. I want you to remember the beginning sound for your word." *(Point to the first child.)* "Your word is *lady*. Your job is to remember the first sound in the word *lady*. (Point to the second child.)* "Your word is *ant*. Your job is to remember the first sound in the word *ant*. (Point to the third child.)* Your word is *pumpkin*. Your job is to remember the first sound in the word *pumpkin*. Let's make a new word." *(Point to each child and have each say his or her sound: /l/ /a/ /p/.)* "If we put those sounds together: /l/ /a/ /p/, what word would we make? *Lap*. That's correct!"

Continue the same process for the following:

1. kitten	animal	top	=	cat
2. add	kite	sock	=	ax
3. mitten	and	dog	=	mad
4. tug	ask	puppy	=	tap

INDEPENDENT PRACTICE ■

"Let's do an activity page and practice this. Let's look at the pictures on the left. These pictures, from left to right, are:

clock	ax	nickel
horseshoe	ant	tools
apple	dog	
light	arrow	pizza
dollars	ashes	mitt

Take the first sound in each picture. Blend the sounds together and make a new word. Then draw a line to the new word pictured in the right-hand column."

REVIEW ■

(Check the activity page together.) "Today we made new words by blending. All of the words had what sound in the middle? Absolutely right—an /a/!"

PREVIEW ■

"Tomorrow, we will work with a new sound, which ends the words *sniff* and *loaf*. Does anyone know what sound we will work on tomorrow? Yes, it's the /f/ sound."

Name _____

Say each picture name across the row on the left. Take the beginning sounds and blend them together to make a new word. Draw a line to the new word in the column on the right.

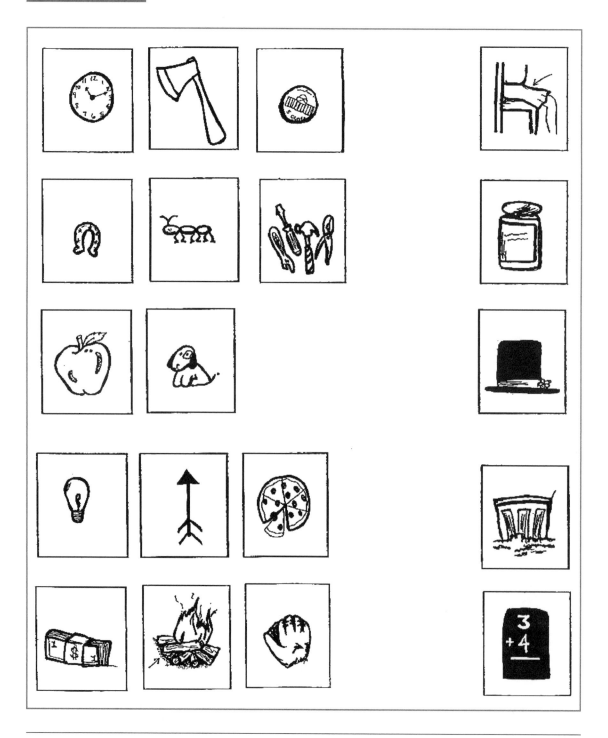

Lesson 10

Recall and Segmentation /f/

OBJECTIVE: *Students will be able to recall words with the initial /f/ phoneme and elongate the phoneme.*

MATERIALS: *music to "Farmer in the Dell" (optional)*

REVIEW ■

"Who can tell me what we have been working on with sounds in words?" *(Give appropriate feedback, and review any previously mastered content.)* "Listen to these words and tell me if the /f/ sound comes at the beginning or end of the word: graph . . . fox . . . self." *(Allow students time between words to respond.)*

PREVIEW ■

"Today we are going to sing a /f/ sound and play a game with the /f/ sound."

PRESENTATION/INSTRUCTION ■

"Who knows the song "The Farmer in the Dell"? Let's sing the first verse to get the tune." *(Sing, hum, or play the song to acquaint the students with the tune.)* "We are going to sing this song, but we will call it "The Fffffarmer in the Fffffield," and he will take a lot of things that start with the /f/ sound. So before we start, you need to think of several /f/ words, because I will call on each one of you to tell me a /f/ word for the song."

GUIDED PRACTICE ■

(Help individual students identify several /f/ words. You may want them to draw a picture of the /f/ word to help with retention for the song.)

The Farmer in the Field
(to the tune of "The Farmer in the Dell")

The fffffffarmer in the fffffield

The ffffffarmer in the fffffield

/F/-/F/-/F/-/F/-/F/-/F/,

The ffffffarmer in the fffield.

The ffffffarmer takes a (*Point to a child for a /f/ word.*)

The ffffffarmer takes a (*Point to a child for a /f/ word.*)

/F/-/F/-/F/-/F/-/F/-/F/,

The ffffffarmer takes a (*Point to a child for a /f/ word.*)

(*Repeat until all the children get to give a /f/ word for the song.*)
(*Last verse*)

The /f/ stands alone

The /f/ stands alone

/F/-/F/-/F/-/F/-/F/-/F/,

The /f/ stands alone.

■ INDEPENDENT PRACTICE

"Great singing. If you didn't get to tell me all of your /f/ words, keep them a secret, because we are going to play a game and you will need to know as many /f/ words as you can.

"Everyone sit cross-legged in a circle. You are going to go around the circle and come up with new /f/ words in this game. You will go around the circle taking turns giving a /f/ word. In between each /f/ word, slap your knees twice, clap twice, snap your fingers on one hand, then snap the fingers on the other hand." (*Demonstrate.*) "If you can't think of a new /f/ word, you say 'FOOIE!' The last ffffour to say 'FOOIE!' will be named the Ffffabulous /f/ Ffffinders."

■ REVIEW

"What new /f/ words did we learn today?"

■ PREVIEW

"Tomorrow we will continue to work on the /f/ sound."

Lesson 11

Identification /f/

OBJECTIVE: *Students will identify the /f/ phoneme in initial and final positions in words.*

MATERIALS: *scissors, paste or glue sticks, and Activity Page F-1 (optional /f/ counters like fish or flies)*

REVIEW ■

"Who can tell me what we have been working on?" *(Review /d/, /s/, and /a/. Give appropriate feedback.)*

PREVIEW ■

"Today we are going to work with the /f/ sound. Everyone, what letter makes the /f/ sound?"

PRESENTATION/INSTRUCTION ■

"Everyone make the /f/ sound. Feel the air squish between your upper teeth and bottom lip? I want you to turn to your neighbor and make the mouth shape for either /f/, /s/, or /a/ . . . *but* don't make the sound. Your neighbor will guess what sound you are making without hearing the sound. Take turns until you have both made all three sounds." *(Give feedback to individuals.)* "Is it easy to tell what sound would come out of the mouth from just the mouth position?"

GUIDED PRACTICE ■

"Let's listen to a story that has lots of /f/ words. Some of the words begin with the /f/ sound and some end with the /f/ sound. I want you to raise your hand every time you hear the /f/ sound. Put up one finger if the /f/ comes in the beginning of the word and two fingers if the /f/ comes at the end of the word. *(If you have /f/ counters, the students can use the counters instead of using their fingers.)* Are you ready?"

Ralph the Elf

I know an <u>elf</u> named <u>Ralph</u>, who lives on a <u>farm</u>. His home is on the <u>leaf</u> of a <u>fine</u> <u>fruit</u> tree. On hot days, he swims in the <u>fountain</u> and <u>fans</u> <u>himself</u> with a <u>feather</u>. <u>Life</u> is <u>fine</u> for <u>Ralph</u> the <u>elf</u>.

(Now go through the story slowly and identify each /f/ sound and its position in the word—beginning or end.)

■ INDEPENDENT PRACTICE

"We are going to do an activity page. All of the words either begin or end with the /f/ sound. You will paste the fish head under the picture if it begins with /f/ or paste the fish tail under the picture if it ends with the /f/ sound. If the first picture was of a ferret, what would you paste under the picture? The fish head, because *ferret* begins with the /f/ sound. If the picture was of a giraffe, what picture would you paste? The tail, because *giraffe* ends with the /f/ sound. Any questions? Put your finger on the picture as I say it: farm, cuff, football; golf, loaf, fountain."

■ REVIEW

(Check activity page together.) "Tell me one word that begins or ends with the /f/ sound." *(Give each child the opportunity to give a word. If they can't remember one, have another student act out the /f/ word while that student guesses.)*

■ PREVIEW

"Tomorrow we will work with a new sound."

Name _____

Cut out the pictures of the fish heads and tails at the bottom of the page. Paste a fish head under each picture that begins with /f/, and paste a tail under each picture that ends with /f/.

Activity Page F-1

Lesson 12

Rhyming /o/

OBJECTIVE: Students will be able to make /o/ rhyming words using word families.

MATERIALS: pencil and paper

■ **REVIEW**

"Who can tell me what we have been working on with sounds in words? What was the last vowel we worked on? Yes, it was /a/. Let's name some /a/ words." *(Give appropriate feedback.)*

■ **PREVIEW**

"Today we are going to work on a new vowel sound. The sound is /o/. Does anyone know what letter makes the /o/ sound most often? Great! We're going to use the /o/ sound to make rhymes."

■ **PRESENTATION/INSTRUCTION**

"The /o/ sound is the first sound you hear in the word *octopus*. Everyone make the /o/ sound. See how the mouth position is different than for the /a/ sound? Who can tell us some more words that begin with the /o/ sound? Great! Now, let's see if we can make some /o/ rhyming words. A rhyme is a word pattern. It is just like a number, shape, or color pattern. If I drew this on the board, what would come next? Yes, a circle.

"How did you know that? You looked at what had come before and continued the pattern. A rhyme is a sound pattern. To rhyme, you take off the beginning sound, keep the last vowel and the rest of the word, and change the beginning sound. In the word *mop*, what's the beginning sound? It's /m/. Take off the /m/ and what is left? . . . 'op.' If I put a /t/ on the beginning of *op*, I'd make the word *top*." *(Blend /t/ and* op *together slowly to make the word* top.) "The words *mop* and *top* rhyme."

GUIDED PRACTICE ■

"Let's go through the alphabet and see if we can add other sounds at the beginning of *op* to make new words." *(Have the students say the sounds associated with each letter of the alphabet and decide if, when added to* op, *it makes a new word.)*

INDEPENDENT PRACTICE ■

"I am going to say a word. Each word will have the /o/ sound in the middle of it. Then I will give you three minutes to write as many words as you can that rhyme with my word. Don't worry about the spelling; it is the sounds that count. Remember to keep the /o/ sound and the last sound, and add a new beginning sound. Use the alphabet for help with new beginning sounds. When I say *stop*, you will put your pencils down. Then you will count the number of words you have written and write that number in the right-hand corner of your paper. We will go around the room and check the /o/ rhyming words. Each person will say one word on his or her list. If the word is correct, everyone who has written that word will get one point. We will continue this until all the words have been said. When we check, you need to listen carefully to see if your words have been said. We will total the points to get Rhyme Time Points." *(Give words: pot, fox, log, cob.)*

REVIEW ■

"Who can tell us how to make a rhyme? Why do you think rhymes are sound patterns?"

PREVIEW ■

"Tomorrow we will work with more /o/ words."

Segmentation /o/

OBJECTIVE: *Students will be able to count the number of phonemes heard in words containing the /o/ sound.*

MATERIALS: *pencils and Activity Page O-1*

■ **REVIEW**

"Who can tell me what we have been working on with sounds in words? Tell me one thing you learned about rhymes yesterday." *(Give appropriate feedback.)*

■ **PREVIEW**

"Today we are going to learn to count sounds in words that have the /o/ sound."

■ **PRESENTATION/INSTRUCTION**

"Remember when we first started learning about sounds? We found out that some words have a lot of sounds and some words have only a few. When you say a word, if you listen carefully, you can hear all the sounds in the word. If I said the word *cot* slowly, *cooooo ot*, c . . . ooooo . . . t, I hear three sounds. I hear /c/" *(hold up one finger)*, "/o/" *(hold up two fingers)*, "/t/" *(hold up three fingers)*. "It is important to think only about the sounds in the word, because if you think of the number of letters, you might get the wrong answer." *(Write the word* are *on the board.)* "What is this word? Everyone say the word *are*. Now stretch it out. Hold up that many fingers." *(As a rule, a vowel followed by* r *is considered to be one sound. However, depending on how you pronounce the word* are *it will have either one or two sounds. Use the number that you feel comfortable with.)* "Everyone who has only one finger up is correct. The word *are* has only one sound, but it has three letters. Often letters will be silent, or when they come together they will make only one sound. Listen: *shot.* Shhhhhh . . . oooooo . . . t. How many sounds do you hear?" *(Take guesses from students.)* "You hear three sounds in shhhhh . . . oooooo . . . t. The letters *s* and *h*, do not say /s/ and /h/. They only make one sound—/sh/."

GUIDED PRACTICE   ■

"Let's do some words together. First we say the words in a stretched way. Then we pause between each sound, watching for our mouth positions to change. Finally we say the word stopping between sounds while using our fingers to count the sounds. Ready? The first word is *lot.* Stretch it out: *lllllllooooot.*

"Now use your fingers: /l/   /o/   /t/   How many sounds in *lot?* Three!"

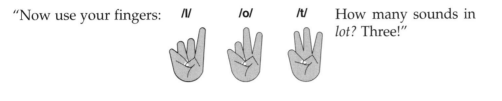

(Use the same procedure to do the following words: hog, mob, odd, and stop.)

INDEPENDENT PRACTICE   ■

"Now we are going to practice counting sounds. Look at the activity page. Let's say the words for the pictures going across each row: *on, cot, olive, pop, octopus, hop, pot, ostrich, log.*"

REVIEW   ■

"Tell me some things you learned about counting sounds."

PREVIEW   ■

"Tomorrow we will use sound counting to play a game."

Name _____

Write the number of sounds you hear in each word under the picture.

Activity Page 0-1

Identification /o/ /a/

OBJECTIVE: The students will distinguish between the /a/ and /o/ vowel phonemes and count the number of phonemes in the word.

MATERIALS: chalkboard and chalk

REVIEW ■

"Who can tell me one thing you have learned about sounds and why that is important?" (*Give appropriate feedback.*) "What sounds have we learned?"

PREVIEW ■

"Today we are going to continue counting sounds and play a sound game."

PRESENTATION/INSTRUCTION ■

"Let's review the two vowel sounds we have worked on, the /o/ sound and the /a/ sound. I am going to make the mouth position for one of the vowels, but I won't make any sound." (*Make the mouth position of /a/.*) "What sound am I making? Everyone! Did you say /a/? Yes! What about this mouth position?" (*Make the mouth position of /o/.*) "Everyone! Terrific, that was the /o/ position. How was my mouth alike both times?" (*Write comments on the board, such as: mouth open, can see inside your mouth, etc.*) "How was it different?" (*Write comments, such as: /a/ mouth stretched back more, etc.*) "What word do you think of to help you remember the /a/ sound?" (*apple, animal, etc.*) "What word helps you remember the /o/ sound?" (*octopus, ostrich, etc.*) "Now let's see who can remember how to count sounds. Before we practice, tell me some rules to remember?" (*Don't think about the spelling, say the word slowly, hold your fingers up to keep track of the sounds.*)

GUIDED PRACTICE ■

"Let's do some words together. Hold up your fingers to count the number of sounds you hear. Ready . . . *chop*. Stretch it out: /ch/ /o/ /p/. Now use your fingers: /ch/" (*one finger*), "/o/" (*two fingers*), "/p/" (*three fingers*).

"How many sounds in *chop*? Three! What vowel did you hear?" (*Use the same procedure to do the following words: dog (3), apple (3), ask (3), mouth (3), add (2).*)

■ INDEPENDENT PRACTICE

"I can see you are ready to play the game. We will divide into two teams and have a relay race. The players at the front of each line will come to the chalkboard and get a piece of chalk. When I say the word, you write down the number of sounds you hear in that word and turn around. The first one with the correct number to turn around gets two points. Then I will ask both players to tell what vowel they heard. Both players will make the mouth shape for the vowel sound without any sound. If both make the correct position, both will get an extra point. Okay!"

off (2)	lamp (4)	brother (5)	otter (3)	wall (3)	father (4)
sock (3)	spot (4)	off (2)	swan (4)	robin (5)	flag (4)
on (2)	office (4)	can (3)	glass (4)	sack (3)	block (4)
hot (3)	trash (4)	as (2)	master (5)	hog (3)	at (2)

■ REVIEW

"Great game! What vowels did you work on?"

■ PREVIEW

"Tomorrow we will work on a new sound."

Lesson 15

Blending /m/

OBJECTIVE: Students will blend phonemes to make words using the /m/ phoneme.

MATERIALS: music to "If You're Happy and You Know It" (optional)

REVIEW ■

"Who can name all of the sounds we have worked on?" *(Give appropriate feedback, and review any previously mastered content.)*

PREVIEW ■

"Today, we are going to work with a new sound. It is the /m/ sound. We'll also play a game."

PRESENTATION/INSTRUCTION ■

"We have been working with a lot of sounds, and you have become really good sound listeners. I am going to give you the sounds today, and you will make the words. All of the words will have the /m/ sound in them. Some will have the /m/ sound at the beginning, and some will have the /m/ sound at the end. Before we start, let's practice making the /m/ sound. Look at your neighbor. How does his or her mouth look?" *(Write comments on the board.)* "Marvelous!"

GUIDED PRACTICE ■

"Let's see if you can solve some /m/ mysteries. What word am I saying: /m/ /a/ /t/? Everyone together." *(Say the sounds separately and have them blend the sounds and call out the word. Use the same procedure to blend the words: ham, mail, milk, ram, map, and marble.)*

INDEPENDENT PRACTICE ■

"Magnificent! You're all ready to sing. Who knows the song, 'If You're Happy and You Know It'? Let's hum it with the /m/ sound. The words to this song go:"

If you think you know this word, raise your hand. *(raise your hand and go "/m/,/m/")*

If you think you know this word, raise your hand. *(raise your hand and go "/m/,/m/")*

If you think you know this word, if you think you know this word,

If you think you know this word, raise your hand. *(raise your hand and go "/m/, /m/")*

(Teacher only: "/m/ /a/ /s/ /k/." Students call out "mask." Repeat for: arm, room, man, moon, mop, limb.)

■ REVIEW

"I want everyone to think of a word that either begins or ends with the /m/ sound." *(Call on all students to give an /m/ word.)*

■ PREVIEW

"Tomorrow, we will do some more work with /m/!"

Segmentation and Identification /m/

OBJECTIVE: *Students will be able to count the number of phonemes in words containing the /m/ phoneme and identify the position of the /m/ phoneme.*

MATERIALS: *M&M's™ candies for all the students (about 20 for each student)*

REVIEW ■

"Who can tell me what we worked with last?" *(Give appropriate feedback, and review any previously mastered content.)*

PREVIEW ■

"Today, we will work with /m/ again."

PRESENTATION/INSTRUCTION ■

"Last time, we blended the /m/ words when I said the sound. Was it easy to pick out the /m/ sound? Make the /m/ sound for me! Check your neighbor's mouth position. Can a moth fly in your mouth while you are making the /m/ sound? No, because your lips are closed. Can a candy get in your mouth? No, not even a candy. Hey, can anyone think of a candy that reminds you of the /m/ sound? Did someone say M&M's? They remind me of the /m/ sound. We are going to use M&M's to count sounds in words and tell where the /m/ sound is heard. Let me show you how. If I say *mat*, then I stretch it out, *mmmmaaaat*, then I say each sound: /m/ /a/ /t/, I count three sounds." *(Hold up your fingers and say the sounds slowly.)* "On my table, I put out three M&M's to represent the three sounds. Now if I were to eat the M&M that stood for the /m/ sound, which one would I eat—the beginning, middle, or end?" *(Say /m/ /a/ /t/ again, holding up fingers.)* "I would eat the beginning one, or first one, right? Are you ready to try?"

■ GUIDED PRACTICE

"I will pass out the M&M's. Remember, you may eat only one for each word, and I will tell you when to eat. If you follow directions well, we will all finish the M&M's you are given. I'll say the word. You say it slowly and count the sounds. Then put out that number of M&M's. Don't eat until we have checked the number. Then we'll eat the /m/ M&M.

"Ready? *Room.* How many M&M's?" *(Three.)* "Which one will you eat?" *(The last one.)*

■ INDEPENDENT PRACTICE

"Ready? *Mouse.* How many M&M's?" *(Three—as the ou [ow] sound is considered one.)* "Which one will you eat?" *(The first one.)*

(Repeat the process for: drum [4], arm [2], marble [4], mountain [6], ram [3], slim [4], me [2], mean [3], worm [3], Monday [5], money [4], farm [3], magic [5]).

"Now let's eat the rest of our M&M's!"

■ REVIEW

"Magnificent! Everyone make the /m/ sound. Those candies were /m/ /m/ good!"

■ PREVIEW

"I think we'll learn a new sound tomorrow."

Lesson 17

Deletion /r/

OBJECTIVE: *Students will delete initial /r/ sound to form new words.*

MATERIALS: *colors* (crayons or markers) *and Activity Page R-1*

REVIEW ■

"Who can tell me what sound we worked on yesterday?" *(Give appropriate feedback, and review any previously mastered content.)*

PREVIEW ■

"Today, we are going to work with a new sound."

PRESENTATION/INSTRUCTION ■

"This sound makes an /r/ like a dog growling. Who knows what letter makes the /r/ sound? Right, it's *r*! I'd like everyone to make the /r/ sound while I check to see if your mouth position is correct." *(Give individual feedback and correction.)* "Great! Now let's say some /r/ words and stretch out the /r/ sound at the beginning of each word. Everyone say the word after I do, stretching out the beginning /r/ sound. *Rrrrrrabbit... rrrrrrobot... rrrrribon... rrrrrright.* Now let's practice taking off the /r/ sound and finding new words that are left. Listen carefully as I show you how. The first word is *rake*. Let's see: *rrraaak, rrr... ake, /r/ake*. Now if I take off the /r/: /r/... *ake*, I'd have the word *ache* left. Does everyone see how I did that? Let's try one together."

GUIDED PRACTICE ■

"The word is *raid*. Let's stretch out the /r/. *Rrraaad*. Let's say that together: /r/ /a/ /d/. Now let's pause after the /r/ sound: /r/... *aid*. What word is left? Everyone? Yes, the word *aid* is left." *(Use the same procedure to do the following words.)*

| rate—ate | rare—air | reach—each | rat—at |

■ INDEPENDENT PRACTICE

"We are going to do an activity page, but you must follow along with me and listen to finish it correctly. See the numbers at the top of the page? I want you to use your crayons to color the numbers certain colors. You must listen to see which number will be what color. Color the number one red, two blue, three yellow, four green, five purple, six brown, seven orange, and eight black." *(You may want to have the students circle the number with that color or have this already done to save time.)* "Now listen carefully. I will say a number and a word. You will pick up the color for the number I just said, then listen to the word. Take the /r/ sound off the beginning of the word to find the word that is left, and color that picture with the color you have in your hand. If I said *five*, what color would you pick up? Purple, correct! Now if I said *rink*, what would you color purple? The picture of the ink. Great listening. Ready, let's color!"

One, *rock* = red, ox	Five, *rink* = purple, ink
Two, *real* = blue, eel	Six, *rod* = brown, odd
Three, *rice* = yellow, ice	Seven, *rich* = orange, itch
Four, *roar* = green, oar	Eight, *race* = black, ace

■ REVIEW

"Today, we worked with the /r/ sound. Everyone make that sound. We sound like angry dogs!"

■ PREVIEW

"Tomorrow, we will work with /r/ again."

Name _____

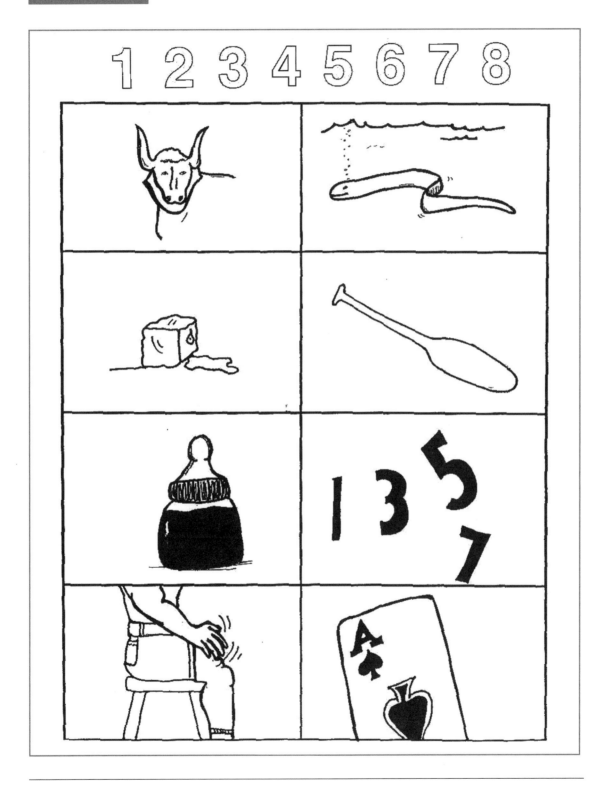

Recall /r/

OBJECTIVE: Students will recall words that begin with the /r/ phoneme.

MATERIALS: pencils, white paper, and music to "Old McDonald" (optional)

■ REVIEW

"What sound starts the words ring, radio, and rooster? Everybody?"

■ PREVIEW

"Today we will continue with the /r/ sound and sing a song, so you'll need to remember as many /r/ words as you can."

■ PRESENTATION/INSTRUCTION

"Let's review some of the sounds we have learned. I'll give you three words, and you tell me what sound the word begins or ends with. Ready?"

dinosaur, dragon, dog	"Begin with what sound?"	mouse, dice, fox	"End with what sound?"
apple, astronaut, ant	"Begin with what sound?"	rose, rat, rope	"Begin with what sound?"
pear, door, star	"End with what sound?"	elf, golf, leaf	"End with what sound?"
rocket, rake, raccoon	"Begin with what sound?"	air, writer, jar	"End with what sound?"

"Let's all make the /r/ sound together. Check your neighbor's mouth position with mine." *(Give individual feedback.)* "Who can demonstrate the correct /r/ position? Where is your tongue in your mouth? I'll say some words, and you raise your hand if the words begin with the /r/ sound: *wagon, rice, rent, turn, car, record, turtle, wonder.* Great!"

GUIDED PRACTICE   ■

"We have been talking about the /r/ sound. Now I want you to draw a picture of as many things as you can think of that begin with the /r/ sound. You don't need to color the picture, because you are going to have only five minutes to finish your picture. Then we will use the picture to help us sing a song. When you finish your picture, I want you to give it to your neighbor to check. Your neighbor will name all the things he or she sees and make sure they all begin with the /r/ sound. Let's brainstorm some /r/ words to get you started. Who can give me an /r/ word?" (*Ask for two or three words, and draw pictures that represent them on the board.*) "Remember, your pictures don't have to be perfect.

"Now you can use these and add some more on your paper."

INDEPENDENT PRACTICE   ■

"Do you all know the song "Old McDonald"? We are going to sing a song to that tune about Ronnie Roster. It goes:

Ronnie Roster had a room, /r/ /r/ /r/ /r/ /r/.

And in his room he had a (*Point to a child to give an /r/ word*), /r/ /r/ /r/ /r/ /r/.

With a (*Point to a child to give an /r/ word*) here,

And a (*Point to a child to give an /r/ word*) there,

Here a (*Point to a child to give an /r/ word*),

There a (*Point to a child to give an /r/ word*),

Everywhere a (*Point to a child to give an /r/ word, point to another child to give another /r/ word*),

Ronnie Roster had a room, /r/ /r/ /r/ /r/ /r/.

(*Repeat song until everyone has a chance to give at least two words.*)

REVIEW   ■

"What sound ends the words *car*, *ear*, and *four*? Everyone make that sound."

PREVIEW   ■

"Who can guess what new vowel sound we will work on next time?" (*Identify the short /e/ sound.*)

Identification /e/

OBJECTIVE: *Students will be able to identify words containing the /e/ phoneme and distinguish between /a/, /o/, and /e/.*

MATERIALS: *pencils, scissors, paste or glue stick, and Activity Page E-1*

■ REVIEW

"Who can tell me what vowels we have worked on?" (*Give appropriate feedback.*)

■ PREVIEW

"Today we are going to work with the sound that begins the word *elephant*. What sound do you hear at the beginning of *elephant?*"

■ PRESENTATION/INSTRUCTION

"Let's all make the /e/ sound. Who can describe my mouth position?" (*Write comments on the board.*) "Let's review the two other vowel sounds we have worked on. The /o/ sound and the /a/ sound. I am going to make the mouth position for one of the three vowels, but I won't make any sound." (*Make the mouth position of /o/.*) "What sound am I making? Everyone! Did you say /o/? Yes! What about this mouth position?" (*Make the mouth position of /e/.*) "Everyone! Terrific, that was the /e/ position. What about this one?" (*Make the mouth position of /a/.*) "Which two look the most alike? Why?" (*Write comments such as: /a/ mouth stretched back more, etc.*) "What word do you think of to help you remember the /a/ sound?" (*apple, animal, etc.*) "What word helps you remember the /o/ sound?" (*octopus, ostrich, etc.*) "I remember the /e/ sound with words such as *elephant, elf,* and *egg.* Make the /e/ sound again and listen carefully. Does anyone have another word that begins with the /e/ sound?"

■ GUIDED PRACTICE

"We are going to listen for the /e/ sound in the middle of words. I'll read a story, and you put a tally mark on your paper every time you hear an

/e/ word, then count your marks and put the number at the top of your page." *(Use the back of the activity page for this activity.)*

Deb and Nell

Deb and Nell are red hens. They live in a pen with ten friends. One day some men came to send Nell away. "Help! Help!" yelled Nell. "Let my friend go!" said Deb. Nell ran like a jet, and the men weren't seen again.

"How many words did you count that had an /e/ in the middle? Put your number on the top of your paper and circle it." *(Now go through the story slowly and make a mark on the chalkboard for each /e/ sound. Count the marks and reward the correct answers.)*

INDEPENDENT PRACTICE ■

"Now let's practice picking out words with the /a/, /o/, and /e/ vowel sounds. Look at the activity page. The pictures are: net, web, ham, top, box; ten, log, hen, ram, cat; dog, lamp, wet, nap, and frog. Paste the apple, octopus, or egg in the box below each picture for the correct vowel sound." *(Correct papers together.)*

REVIEW ■

"Today, we worked with the new vowel sound /e/ and reviewed /a/ and /o/."

PREVIEW ■

"We are going to work with the /e/ sound again tomorrow."

Name _____

Paste the picture of the apple, octopus, or egg under each picture to show the correct vowel sound.

Activity Page E-1

Identification and Recall /e/

OBJECTIVE: *Students will recall words that contain the /e/ phoneme using phoneme and content clues.*

MATERIALS: *pencil, paper, and chalkboard*

REVIEW ■

"Who can tell me what we have been working on with sounds in words?" *(Give appropriate feedback, and review any previously mastered content.)*

PREVIEW ■

"Today, we are going to guess /e/ words and make our own riddles."

PRESENTATION/INSTRUCTION ■

"Who can tell me the three vowels we have learned? Let's practice making the correct mouth positions for each." *(Give individual feedback.)* "The vowels /a/ and /e/ are tricky, because the mouth positions look a lot alike. It is easier to remember if you have a word to help you. I use *apple* for /a/, because if I act as if I am taking a big bite out of an apple" *(act as if you are taking a bite of an apple)* "and say aaaaaaaapple, my mouth will make the /a/ position. Let's all do that. Great. I use the word *egg* to help me remember /e/, because my mouth position looks like an egg." *(Make the /e/ position.)* "Do you see that? Using mouth positions will help you decide what sound is in a word."

GUIDED PRACTICE ■

"Let's practice making a riddle for an /e/ word. Let's brainstorm some /e/ words." *(Have the group decide the one for which to make a riddle.)* "Now let's make some clues." *(Write responses on the board.)* "What sound does the word start with? Where is the /e/ sound? How many sounds are in the word? What are some things that describe this word? Now, let's number these clues from the easiest to the hardest. We will put the hard clues first and the easier clues last to make the riddle more fun."

■ INDEPENDENT PRACTICE

"Now that you know how to make a riddle, let's see if you can figure out my riddles. I'm going to give you clues to a word. That word will have the /e/ sound in it somewhere. I'm going to divide the class into teams. After each clue, your team will have a chance to guess. You will get one point for every /e/ word you guess, even if it is not the correct word. If you say a word that doesn't have an /e/, your team will lose two points. The team that guesses the correct word first gets three points." (*Teams take turns guessing first. Stop taking guesses when the correct word has been identified, and give out points. Let the team guess only once after a clue is given. After one guess they must wait until the next clue is given to guess again.*)

- I'm thinking of a word that begins with the /e/ sound. (*Take guesses.*)
- It has three sounds all together. (*Take guesses.*)
- It is a kind of animal. (*Take guesses.*)
- The last sound is /k/. (*Take guesses.*)
- It is a member of the deer family. (*Take guesses.*)
- It has antlers. (*Take guesses.*)
- The middle sound is /l/. (*Take guesses.*)

ELK

- I'm thinking of a word that begins with the /f/ sound. (*Take guesses.*)
- The /e/ sound is second in the word. (*Take guesses.*)
- It has a total of four sounds. (*Take guesses.*)
- It is found outside. (*Take guesses.*)
- People have them in their yards. (*Take guesses.*)
- The last sound in the word is /s/. (*Take guesses.*)
- They keep animals and people in. (*Take guesses.*)

FENCE

- I'm thinking of a word that begins with the /s/ sound. (*Take guesses.*)
- It has a total of three sounds. (*Take guesses.*)
- The /e/ comes in the middle. (*Take guesses.*)
- It means to talk. (*Take guesses.*)
- The last sound is /d/. (*Take guesses.*)
- It is the past tense of the second word in the game, Simon . . . (*Take guesses.*)

SAID

- I'm thinking of a word that begins with the /e/ sound. (*Take guesses.*)
- The last sound is /o/. (*Pronounced long o. Take guesses.*)
- These people live in a cold place. (*Take guesses.*)
- The second sound is /s/. (*Take guesses.*)

- Many used to live in igloos. (Take guesses.)
- They live in Alaska. The second sound is /s/. (Take guesses.)

ESKIMO

- I'm thinking of a word that begins with the /l/ sound. *(Take guesses.)*
- The /e/ comes second. *(Take guesses.)*
- It is something you eat. *(Take guesses.)*
- It is yellow. *(Take guesses.)*
- You can make a drink out of it. *(Take guesses.)*
- It is sour. *(Take guesses.)*

LEMON

- I'm thinking of a word that has an /e/ in the second place. *(Take guesses.)*
- It is a body part. *(Take guesses.)*
- It ends with a /d/ sound. *(Take guesses.)*
- It sits on your shoulders. *(Take guesses.)*

HEAD

"Now I want your team to make up three more riddles just like the ones I have done. Remember, all of the words must have the /e/ sound in them somewhere. Then you will get to give your riddles to the other team. If they guess correctly on the first guess, they get 10 points, second guess they get 9 points, and so on." *(Give each team time to make the new riddles. Add these points to the team score.)*

REVIEW ◼

"What sound did we work on today? Everyone make that sound using correct mouth position."

PREVIEW ◼

"Tomorrow, we will play another /e/ game."

Segmentation /e/

OBJECTIVE: Students will count the number of sounds in words containing the /e/ phoneme.

MATERIALS: none

■ REVIEW

"What sound begins elephant, egg, and Eskimo? Yes, we have been working on the /e/ vowel sound." (*Give appropriate feedback, and review any previously mastered content.*)

■ PREVIEW

"I think you are ready to play a game with /e/ words."

■ PRESENTATION/INSTRUCTION

"Does everyone remember how to say words in a stretched way? Listen as I stretch out egg. Eeeeg." (*Say individual phonemes and pause between them: /e/ /g/.*) "How many sounds did you hear in the word egg? Let's use our fingers to keep track: /e/," (*hold up one finger*) "/g/" (*hold up two fingers*). Let's do some more using our fingers."

■ GUIDED PRACTICE

(*Use the same procedure to do the following words together: best—4, hen—3, belt—4, friend—5.*)

■ INDEPENDENT PRACTICE

"I think you are ready to play the game. This game is called Around the Sound. It is like Around the World, but you have to count sounds. We will sit in a circle. Two players will start the game." (*Choose two players.*) "Those two players will stand up. I will say a word. The first player to give the correct number of sounds in the word will move to the next player. The player that makes it around the circle back to his or her same position is the Sound Expert for the Day." *(This game works best with small groups. Ten students are ideal. This allows more engaged time for each student. You may want to use students to be additional word callers to allow for smaller groups. Winners then become the next word caller.)* "Ready? Let's get in a circle. Remember where you are sitting, because the goal of the game is to move around the circle and back to this." *(Pronunciation and dialect will vary the number of phonemes. Use your own judgment about the number of phonemes that are present in each word.)*

Game words:

pet-3	pen-3	fence-4	epidemic-7	enter-4	petal-4
message-5	jet-3	elbow-4	bread-4	ebb-2	ready-4
said-3	record-5	elephant-7	red-3	melon-4	beg-3
Eskimo-5	dress-4	petal-4	check-3	elevator-7	forget-5
memorize-6	desk-4	neck-3	bellow-4	decorate-6	effort-4
extra-6	element-7	led-3	elf-3	exercise-7	heaven-5
kennel-4	negative-7	sled-4	pet-3	represent-9	test-4

REVIEW ■

"What sound begins *extra* and *effort*? Everyone! How do you make that sound?"

PREVIEW ■

"Tomorrow, we will work with a new sound."

Identification and Recall /p/

OBJECTIVE: *Students will identify words with the /p/ phoneme and recall words that contain the /p/ phoneme.*

MATERIALS: *music to "The Wheels on the Bus" (optional), pencil, and paper*

■ REVIEW

"Who can tell me one reason it is good to be able to listen to sounds in words?"

■ PREVIEW

"Today, we are going to work with the sound that ends the word *cup*. What sound is that? It's /p/!"

■ PRESENTATION/INSTRUCTION

"The /p/ sound is special, because your lips make a popping motion. The air shoots out quickly. I remember the /p/ sound by thinking of popcorn. It pops just like your lips do when you make the /p/ sound. Let's all say *pop* together and feel the position your mouth makes for the /p/ sound. Turn to your neighbor and make the /p/ sound. Are your neighbor's lips popping like mine? Hold your hand up in front of your mouth. Can you feel the air come out of your mouth? Great! You are making the correct mouth position for the /p/ sound. I am going to say a long word. Watch my mouth to see if the /p/ sound comes in the beginning, middle, or end. *Rumpelstiltskin.* Now I will say the word again and hold my hand in front of my mouth to feel the /p/ sound." *(Demonstrate.)* "I want everyone to do the same thing. Where did you hear the /p/ sound? Correct, in the middle. Where did you see the /p/ sound when I said the word? Where did you feel the /p/ sound? That trick will help you identify /p/ words. Let's sing a song about the /p/ sound."

GUIDED PRACTICE ■

"Who knows the song 'The Wheels on the Bus'? Let's sing one verse to get the correct tune. Now we are going to change the words to 'The Pigs in the Park.' The pigs are going to jump" (*make jumping motion*), "peek" (*look through your fingers*), "point" (*point finger*), "and tap" (*shuffle your feet*). "The pigs go all through the pasture. Let's all stand up, and we are going to make the motions."

The Pigs in the Park

The pigs in the park go jump, jump, jump

Jump, jump, jump

Jump, jump, jump

The pigs in the park go jump, jump, jump

All through the pasture.

(*Do motions as you sing, and repeat for* peek, point, *and* tap.)

INDEPENDENT PRACTICE ■

"Now that you know how to identify the /p/ sound, I want you to get into groups. Your group must demonstrate the /p/ sound. You could come up with new /p/ action words to 'The Pigs in the Park' song, write a rap, draw a /p/ picture, write a /p/ poem or story, or put on a /p/ play. Hey, what do the words *rap, picture, poem,* and *play* have in common? Where do you hear the /p/ sound? Let's brainstorm some other /p/ words to help get you thinking." (*Write words on the board. Include proper names and names of animals. Give the students time to create. Ask them to share with the class.*)

REVIEW ■

"Tell me what you learned today."

PREVIEW ■

"Tomorrow, we will work with /p/ again."

Lesson 23

Deletion /p/

OBJECTIVE: Students will delete the /p/ phoneme found in either the initial or final position to form a new word.

MATERIALS: note cards with words written on them

■ REVIEW

"Who can tell me some words that begin or end with a /p/ sound?" (*Give appropriate feedback.*)

■ PREVIEW

"We're going to act out some words today."

■ PRESENTATION/INSTRUCTION

"Who can tell me some tricks to remembering the /p/ sound?" (*Lips pop, air comes out quickly, can feel the air with your hand, remember word popcorn.*) "You all had the chance to do a /p/ performance. Today, we are going to take the /p/ sound off of words to make new words. Let me show you how to stretch words out to hear all of the sound. I will stretch out the word *pat*. (*Paaaaat, p . . . aaaa . . . t, /p/ /a/ /t/*). Where is the /p/ sound? Yes, at the beginning. If I take off the /p/ sound, what happens? (*/a/ /t/*) The word *at* is left. Let's do some of these together. The /p/ sound will be either at the beginning or the end."

■ GUIDED PRACTICE

(*Repeat the process above for the words* pace, tarp, pear, pan, ramp, pail, *and* leap.) "Now, I am going to do a charade. You must guess the word." (*Point to your eye and get the students to say "eye."*) "Now put a /p/ at the beginning of that word. What new word did you make? "Pie! Perfect!"

82

INDEPENDENT PRACTICE ■

"You are all going to get the chance to make up your own actions for a game of charades. You will get into groups of two. I will give you and your partner a word. You will take off the /p/ sound and make up an action for the remaining word. Then you will stand in front of the class and act out your word. When we get it, you will tell us if the /p/ comes at the beginning or end, and we will make a new word."

(Following are words to write on note cards. Remember to have the students act out the word after the /p/ is deleted!)

pants	pin	carp	yelp
part	pink	lamp	ramp
poke	play	gasp	soap
peal	pow	beep	sheep

REVIEW ■

"Explain to me how you can take off a sound on a word to make a new word." *(Take comments from several students and have some demonstration of stretching words out.)*

PREVIEW ■

"Tomorrow, we will work with a new sound. Any guesses?" *(Take guesses, and identify sounds you have already done. The next phoneme is /n/.)*

Blending /n/

OBJECTIVE: Students will blend individual phonemes to form words containing the /n/ phoneme.

MATERIALS: music to "Row Row Row Your Boat" (optional)

■ REVIEW

"Who can tell me some sounds we have worked on?" *(Give appropriate feedback, and review any previously mastered content.)*

■ PREVIEW

"Today, we are going to work with the /n/ sound."

■ PRESENTATION/INSTRUCTION

"Everyone make the sound you hear at the beginning of *nice* and *nurse*. Who can tell me what you notice about your mouth position. Your lips are slightly apart and your tongue sits behind your upper teeth. Check your neighbor's mouth position as we all make the /n/ sound." *(Give individual feedback.)* "Yesterday, we worked on breaking words into their sound parts. Today, we are going to make words from sounds. If I said /n/ /u/ /t/ then blended it into a stretched form *nnnnuuuut*, I would make the word *nut*. It is important to be able to blend because if you are reading a new word and you know the sounds, you have to put the sounds together to say the word."

■ GUIDED PRACTICE

"Let's practice some. I'll say the sounds. You tell me what word it would make blended together. All of the words will have the /n/ sound somewhere in them. Ready?" *(Say sounds, pausing between each one.)*

/f/ /a/ /n/	Everybody . . . "fan"	/n/ /e/ /c/	Everybody . . . "neck"
/n/ /i/ /c/ /l/	Everybody . . . "nickel"	/ch/ /i/ /k/ /n/	Everybody . . . "chicken"
/d/ /e/ /n/ /t/	Everybody . . . "dent"	/m/ /oo/ /n/	Everybody . . . "moon"

INDEPENDENT PRACTICE ■

"Now let's sing a song. Who knows 'Row, Row, Row Your Boat'? Let's sing one verse. In the new song we are going to /n/ /o/ /d/ your body parts to the tune of 'Row, Row, Row Your Boat.' You will know what to move by blending together sounds to make a word. Ready?"

/n/ /o/ /d/ Your Nose (Nod your Nose)

/n/ /o/ /d/ your . . . /n/ /o/ /z/ (nose) *(Pause, pronouncing each phoneme of the body part)*

Gently up and down, *(Have students try to wiggle their noses)*

Neatly, neatly, neatly, nest,

Do your very best!

(Repeat the same procedure for: Nod your knee, Nod your hand, Nod your neck, Nod your noggin, and Nod your shin.)

REVIEW ■

"Everyone give yourself a pat on the back, and tell me what word this is: /f/ /i/ /n/. Yes, you did a *fine* job today!"

PREVIEW ■

"We will also do the /n/ sound tomorrow."

Identification /n/

OBJECTIVE: Students will identify words with the /n/ phoneme in the final position.

MATERIALS: scissors and N-1 Activity Pages (one set for every two students copied onto tagboard)

■ REVIEW

"Who can tell me what sound we are working on?" *(Give appropriate feedback.)*

■ PREVIEW

"Today, we are going to find words that have the /n/ sound at the end of the word."

■ PRESENTATION/INSTRUCTION

"Remember yesterday? You blended to get new words. Today, you will need to break down words to find where the /n/ sound comes. What mouth position would we look for?" *(Write comments on the board.)* "I will come around to check your mouth position, so everyone take a deep breath and make the /n/ sound." *(Circulate and give feedback.)* "Nice! That word begins with the /n/ sound. I know because I can feel my tongue touch the back of my upper teeth at the beginning of that word. *Fin* ends with the /n/ sound because my tongue goes up last. Let's say some words and see if you can find out where the /n/ sound comes."

■ GUIDED PRACTICE

"I'll say the word. You repeat it. Hold up one finger if you hear the /n/ at the beginning of the word and two fingers if you hear it at the end of the word. Ready?"

neck	note
learn	begin
nut	between
one	newspaper

INDEPENDENT PRACTICE ■

"Let's play a game doing the same thing. You will get a partner. You and your partner will get a set of cards. Cut the cards apart. You will put the cards face-down in the center and take turns drawing a card and turning it face up on a new pile. When the card is a picture of a word that ends with the /n/ sound, the first person to slap the card gets to keep that card and all the cards under it. Be careful to slap gently or you will lose cards. When all the cards are gone, count your cards to find the winner!" *(Go through the picture cards with the students and go over the picture names before you play the game.)*

N-1 Activity Pages Picture Key

Activity Page N-1a: hen, yarn, pin; corn, spoon, moon; mitten, pumpkin, pan

Activity Page N-1b: barn, kitchen, man; sun, lemon, thorn; crown, train, horn

Activity Page N-1c: fan, pen, lion; note, newspaper, nest; pajamas, pencil, snake

Activity Page N-1d: socks, drums, lamb; Eskimo, horse, nickel; rabbit, brush, bee

Activity Page N-1e: carrot, jar, wave; tube, rose, bass; koala, pot, kangaroo

REVIEW ■

"Who can tell me one word you slapped that ended with the /n/ sound?"

PREVIEW ■

"Tomorrow, we will work on a new sound."

Rhyming /u/

OBJECTIVE: *Students will use word families to make rhyming words containing the /u/ vowel sound.*

MATERIALS: *pencil, paper, and colors (optional for illustrations)*

REVIEW ■

"Who can tell me what vowels we have worked on?" *(Review all previously mastered vowels.)*

PREVIEW ■

"Today, we are going to use what we have learned about word families to make rhyming words. The sound we are going to use to make rhymes starts the words: *umbrella*, *under*, and *up*. Everyone make the sound that we are working on today." *(Students respond /u/.)* "When someone asks you a question that you don't know the answer to, what sound do you make while you are thinking? Does anyone say /u/? Everyone make that sound. Do we sound like we are thinking? Who can describe the mouth position for the /u/ sound? Now, let's see if we can make some /u/ rhyming words. Remember that a rhyme is a word pattern. It is just like a number, shape, or color pattern. If I drew this on the board:

3   6   9   12   *(or any pattern the students would understand)*

"What would come next? Yes, the number 15. How did you know that? You looked at what had come before and continued the pattern. A rhyme is a sound pattern. To rhyme, you take off the beginning sound, keep the vowel and the rest of the word, and change the beginning sound. In the word *bug*, what's the beginning sound? It's /b/. Take off the /b/ and what is left? *Ug*. If I put a /t/ on the beginning of *ug*, I'd make the word *tug*." *(Blend /t/ and "ug" together slowly.)*

GUIDED PRACTICE ■

"Let's do some together. I'll give the word. You take off the first sound and tell what is left. Then, I'll give a new beginning sound, and we will say the words together. Ready? *Cut*. What sound is at the beginning of *cut*? Everyone? /c/. What sound is left when you take the /c/ off? *Ut*. Now put a /m/ at the beginning. What word did you make? Now, put a /g/ sound at the beginning of *ut*. What word did you make? The /h/ sound at the beginning of *ut* would make what word?" *(Follow the same procedure for tub, rub, hub, and cub.)*

Rhyming words are often used at the end of sentences in poems. Listen to the following poem, and try to find all of the rhyming words.

Teddy Bear, Teddy Bear, turn around;

Teddy Bear, Teddy Bear, touch the ground.

Teddy Bear, Teddy Bear, tie your shoe;

Teddy Bear, Teddy Bear, that will do.

(Discuss poem structure.)

■ INDEPENDENT PRACTICE

"Let's brainstorm some action words that have the /u/ sound in them. Then, you will use these words to write your own poem about an animal that you choose. *(Write words in "families" on the board: run, done, fun, sun, ton, bun; hug, bug, tug, lug, snug; jump, stump, etc. Students may illustrate their poems if there is time.)*

■ REVIEW

"Let's all share our poems. The class will listen and pick out the rhyming words."

■ PREVIEW

"Tomorrow, we are going to work on the /u/ sound again."

Segmentation and Identification /u/

OBJECTIVE: Students will draw circles for each phoneme heard in a word then fill in the circle for the /u/ phoneme in each word.

MATERIALS: pencil and paper

REVIEW ■

"Who would like to share two rhyming words you used yesterday in your poem?"

PREVIEW ■

"Today we are going to listen to more /u/ words and sound out the sounds in the words."

PRESENTATION/INSTRUCTION ■

"Let's review how to make the /u/ sound. What does the sound make you think of?" *(What sound do you make when you are thinking?)* "Describe the mouth position. You are ready to practice stretching out /u/ words and counting the sound. I'll show you first. First, I will say the word in the stretched way. Then I will hold up my fingers to count the number of sounds you hear. The first word is *pup*. Stretch it out: *puuuup*.

Now use your fingers: **/p/**   **/u/**   **/p/**   How many sounds in *pup*? Three! The /u/ sound is in the middle."

GUIDED PRACTICE ■

(Use the same procedure with the students to do the following words: stump, some, and butter.)

95

■ INDEPENDENT PRACTICE

"Now I want you to use your paper and pencil. I will say a word. You listen to that word and draw a circle on your paper for each sound you hear. Then you will fill in the circle for the /u/ sound." (*Demonstrate on the board for the word* was.)

1. rug ○ ● ○	7. fussy ○ ● ○ ○
2. because ○ ○ ○ ● ○	8. tug ○ ● ○
3. enough ○ ○ ● ○	9. umpire ● ○ ○ ○
4. jump ○ ● ○ ○	10. bunk ○ ● ○ ○
5. under ● ○ ○ ○	11. stump ○ ○ ● ○
6. summer ○ ● ○ ○	12. butterfly ○ ● ○ ○ ○ ○ ○

■ REVIEW

(*Check papers together and discuss the position of the /u/ in each word. Praise effort.*)

■ PREVIEW

"Tomorrow, we will do a puzzle."

Blending /u/

OBJECTIVE: *Students will blend initial phonemes in picture words to form new words with the /u/ sound in a crossword puzzle.*

MATERIALS: *pencil, paper, scissors, glue, and Activity Pages U-1*

REVIEW ◼

"Who can tell me what vowel sound we are working on?" *(Give appropriate feedback.)*

PREVIEW ◼

"Today we are going to do a puzzle of /u/ words."

PRESENTATION/INSTRUCTION ◼

"Let's review how to make the /u/ sound. Who can share some words that have the /u/ sound in them? Yesterday we counted the sounds in /u/ words. Today, I am going to give you the sounds, and you will make the words. If I heard someone say: /t/ /u/ /b/, I could blend the sounds together to make *tuuub*, which is the word *tub*. *(Demonstrate elongating the sounds then constructing the word.)* "Who can give me some more sounds that will make /u/ words?" *(Have students give individual phonemes in words containing the /u/ sound, while you model the blending to form words.)*

GUIDED PRACTICE ◼

"Now, I will give you the sounds. You blend them into words." *(Pronounce the individual phonemes for: cut, front, sun, and hug.)*

INDEPENDENT PRACTICE ◼

"Now, you are going to do a crossword puzzle. To do the puzzle, you must listen to the clues I will read, and glue the sounds for the words in the correct blanks. Don't glue them into place until you have finished the puzzle, so you can change them if you have made a mistake. Let's do the first one together." *(Demonstrate the concept of across and down. Read the clues. Students guess the word and write it on a separate sheet of paper. See if they can make the word with the pictures, blending the beginning sounds for each picture together to make a new word. For example [turtle] + [umbrella] + [goat] = /t/ /u/ /g/ = tug. You may want the students to work in pairs to complete this activity. You read the clues for the puzzle.)*

Across Clues

1. I start with the /b/ sound. I am something you might carry water in. *bucket*

2. I start and end with the same sound. Tires are made out of me. *rubber*

3. /n/ is my second sound. I mean below. *under*

4. /d/ is my last sound. I am made by mixing dirt and water. *mud*

Down Clues

1. I start with the /b/ sound. I am the opposite of sister. *brother*

2. I end with the /b/ sound. I am a baby bear. *cub*

3. I end with the /m/ sound. You play me. *drum*

4. I start with the /f/ sound. I am what you call a lot of rain. *flood*

Activity Page U-1b Picture Key

bell, cat, diamond, egg, envelope, fish, light, moon, racket, tent, thumb, net, umbrella

■ REVIEW

"Tell me one thing you learned today." *(Ask all students for comments.)*

■ PREVIEW

"Tomorrow, we will work on the sound that begins *turtle*. What sound will we work on tomorrow?"

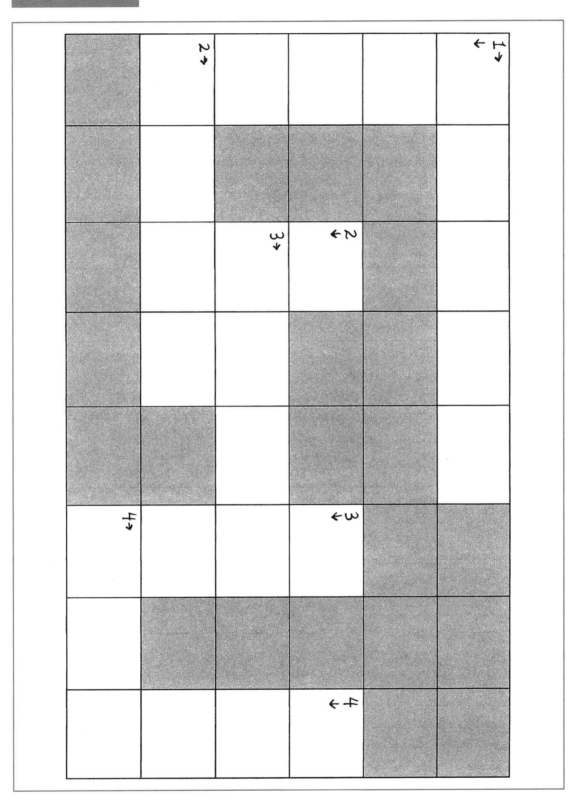

Identification /t/

OBJECTIVE: *Students will be able to identify the /t/ phoneme when heard at the beginning and end of words.*

MATERIALS: *pencil, crayons, and Activity Page T-1*

REVIEW ■

"I want everyone to think of a sound that we have been working on, tell us the sound, and show us the mouth position." (*Give appropriate feedback, and review previously mastered content.*)

PREVIEW ■

"Today we are going to talk about the sound that ends the words *tart, it,* and *heart.* What sound is that?"

PRESENTATION/INSTRUCTION ■

"Let's say the /t/ sound together. Look at my mouth while I make the /t/ sound. This is another sound that makes a puff of air. Who can name a sound that also makes a puff of air?" (*/p/*) "Now turn to a neighbor and make the /t/ sound. Make sure your lips look like mine. Do you think you can pick out /t/ sound in words?"

GUIDED PRACTICE ■

"I am going to say some words that have the /t/ sound in them. We are going to be listening for words that start with the /t/ sound. Everyone use thumbs up or thumbs down to tell me if these words start with the /t/ sound. Remember to watch my mouth."

table	tiger	putter	truck	toe	net

"Now, let's listen for the /t/ sound at the end of words. Everyone use thumbs up or thumbs down to tell me if these words end with the /t/ sound. Remember to watch my mouth."

tools	teeth	wet	nut	turtle	boat

■ INDEPENDENT PRACTICE

"Now I'll read the story. I want you to hold up your hand every time you hear a word that ends with the /t/ sound. I will read the story slowly. Ready?"

Kit the Goat

<u>Kit</u> the <u>Goat</u> was a <u>quaint</u> animal. She liked to <u>float</u> in her <u>boat</u> around her <u>moat</u>. She would <u>sit</u> and <u>sit</u> even when <u>it</u> was <u>hot</u>. She <u>wrote</u> and did <u>art</u> in her <u>boat</u>. When the <u>frost</u> came, she wore a <u>coat</u>, but still she rode in her <u>boat</u>.

"Let's color a picture of that boat." *(Pass out boat activity page.)* "What things will you put in it? Remember to put in things that end with the /t/ sound." *(Tell students not to write the words, but to use pictures to represent the words that end with /t/.)*

■ REVIEW

"Today we learned to listen for the /t/ sound at the end of words. Let's make the /t/ sound. Turn to your neighbor and have them check your mouth position."

■ PREVIEW

"Tomorrow we will work with more /t/ sounds."

Play the Slap, Clap, Snap game with words that end with the /t/ sound.

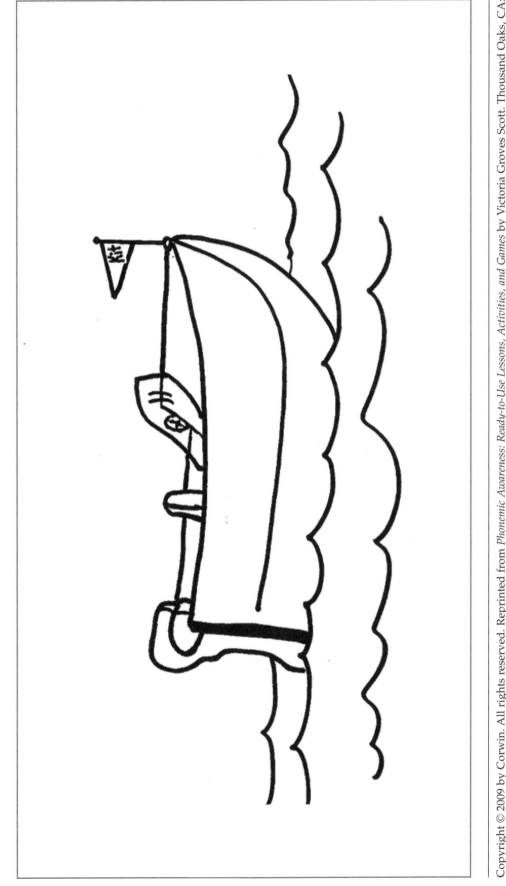

Lesson 30

Deletion /t/

OBJECTIVE: Students will delete the initial or final /t/ phoneme in words to make new words.

MATERIALS: pencil

■ REVIEW

"Who can tell me what sound we were working on?" *(Give appropriate feedback, and review any previously mastered content.)*

■ PREVIEW

"We are going to continue working on the /t/ sound today."

■ PRESENTATION/INSTRUCTION

"Yesterday we learned that the /t/ sound makes a puff of air. I'd like everyone to make the /t/ sound while I check to see if your mouth position is correct." *(Give individual feedback and correction.)* "Great! Now let's say some /t/ words and stretch out the /t/ sound at the beginning of each word, then we will take the /t/ sound off and see what word is left. Listen carefully as I show you how. The first word is *tear (as in cry tears)*. Let's say *teeeerrrr, t . . . ear, /t/ . . . ear*. Now if I take off the /t/: */t/ . . . ear*, I'd have the word *ear* left. Does everyone see how I did that? Let's try one together, but this time let's take off the /t/ sound at the end of the word. The word is *belt*. Let's see: *beeelllt, bell . . . t, bell . . . /t/*. Now if I take off the /t/: *bell . . . /t/*, I'd have the word *bell* left."

■ GUIDED PRACTICE

(Use the same procedure to do the words: tall, art, tax, great, and malt.)

INDEPENDENT PRACTICE ■

"Let's play a game of Simon Says. I'm going to say a word and ask you to take out the /t/ sound. Then everyone will say that word. We will all line up at the back of the room. Every time you get the word correct, you may take one step forward. If you miss the word, you take one step back. I will listen carefully and so will your neighbors, so be responsible moving forward or back on your own. The first people at the front of the room will be the winners. Remember to wait until Simon says to move! Ready? Simon says say *cart* without the /t/. If you said *car*, Simon says take one step up. Simon says say *tar* without the /t/. If you said *are*, take one step up." *(Anyone who moves has to take a step back, because Simon didn't say to move. Repeat this process for:* neat, tin, table, halt, tape, tote [toe or oat], teal, goat, note, teach, boat, tame, *and* tie.*)*

REVIEW ■

"Today, we worked on taking off the /t/ sound in words to make new words. Tell me one word you said where you got to move forward."

PREVIEW ■

"Tomorrow, we will work with a new sound."

Recall /k/

OBJECTIVE: *Students will be able to recall words with the initial or final /k/ phoneme.*

MATERIALS: *music to "The Farmer in the Dell" (optional), blown-up beach ball*

■ REVIEW

"Who can tell me what we have been working on with sounds in words?" *(Give appropriate feedback, and review any previously mastered content.)*

■ PREVIEW

"Today, we are going to work with the sound that ends the words *kick, tack,* and *lock*."

■ PRESENTATION/INSTRUCTION

"We are going to sing a song. Who knows the song "The Farmer in the Dell"? Let's sing the first verse to get the tune." *(Sing, hum, or play the song to acquaint the students with the tune.)* "We are going to sing this song, but we will call it "The Kitten in the Kitchen," and the kitten will take a lot of things that start with the /k/ sound. So before we start, you need to think of several /k/ words, because I will call on each one of you to tell me a /k/ word for the song. Everyone make the /k/ sound. What kind of sound is that? Do you tap, blow, or puff? Yes, the /k/ sound, just like the /t/ sound, is a puffing sound."

■ GUIDED PRACTICE

"Let's brainstorm some /k/ words and draw pictures of them on the board." *(After brainstorming, sing the song.)*

The Kitten in the Kitchen

(sung to the tune of "The Farmer in the Dell")

> The kitten in the kitchen, the kitten in the kitchen,
>
> /k/-/k/-/k/-/k/-/k/-/k/, the kitten in the kitchen.
>
> The kitten takes a (*Point to a child for a /k/ word.*)
>
> The kitten takes a (*Point to a child for a /k/ word.*)
>
> /k/-/k/-/k/-/k/-/k/-/k/, the kitten takes a (*Point to a child for a /k/ word.*)
>
> (*Repeat until all the children get to give a /k/ word for the song.*)

(Last verse)

> The /k/ stands alone. The /k/ stands alone.
>
> /k/-/k/-/k/-/k/-/k/-/k/, the /k/ stands alone.

INDEPENDENT PRACTICE ■

"Great singing. If you didn't get to tell me all of your /k/ words, keep them a secret, because we are going to play a game, and you will need to know as many /k/ words as you can. I will divide you into two teams. Each team member will sit on his or her desk. We are going to play /k/ Volleyball. Here are the rules. You must hit the ball from your side of the room to the other team's side of the room." (*Use a divider, string, or line on the floor to designate room sides.*) "Every time you touch the ball, you must yell a /k/ word. If you don't get to the ball and it hits the floor, if the ball is hit out of bounds, if a player doesn't say a /k/ word, if a player's bottom leaves his or her desk, if the same player hits the ball twice, or if a player repeats a /k/ word, the other team gets a point. Your team may hit the ball twice before it goes over the imaginary net. Remember, everyone on your team should get a chance to play. We will play to 10."

REVIEW ■

"Tell me some /k/ words we used today in the game."

PREVIEW ■

"Tomorrow, we will work with a new sound."

Lesson 32

Segmentation /k/

OBJECTIVE: *Students will be able to count the number of sounds heard in words containing the /k/ phoneme.*

MATERIALS: *scissors and Activity Page K-1*

◼ REVIEW

"Who can tell me one /k/ word you used yesterday?" *(Give appropriate feedback.)*

◼ PREVIEW

"Today, we are going to count sounds in words that have the /k/ sound."

◼ PRESENTATION/INSTRUCTION

"Remember, we found out that some words have a lot of sounds, and some words have only a few. When you say a word, if you listen carefully, you can hear all the sounds in the word. If I say the word *cat* slowly, *caaaaat, c . . . aaaaa . . . t,* I hear three sounds. I hear /c/" *(hold up one finger),* "/a/" *(hold up two fingers),* "/t/" *(hold up three fingers).* It is important to think only about the sounds in the word, because if you think of the number of letters, you might get the wrong answer." *(Write the word rain on the board.)* "What is this word? Everyone say the word *rain.* Now stretch it out. Hold up that many fingers. Everyone that has three fingers up is correct. The word *rain* has only three sounds, but it has four letters. Often letters will be silent, or when they come together, they will make only one sound."

◼ GUIDED PRACTICE

"Let's do some words together and first say them the stretched way. Then we will hold up our fingers to count the number of sounds you hear. Ready? The first word is *kiss.* Stretch it out: *kiiiiissss.*

Now use your fingers: **/k/**   **/i/**   **/s/**   How many sounds in *kiss*? Three!

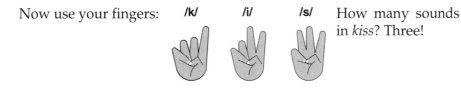

(Use the same procedure to do the following words: beak, camel, cow, candle, peek.*)*

INDEPENDENT PRACTICE   ■

"Now, we are going to play Sound Counting Bingo. Cut up the pictures, and put the cards out in three rows of three. Put the leftover cards into a pile. I will call out the number of sounds and the placement of the /k/ sound—at the beginning, middle, or end of the word. You then find that picture and turn it over. When you get three in a row, you call out 'Sound-O!'" *(Have the students count the sounds and put that number on the line below the picture to make the game go faster. Play several games, allowing them to switch cards. The pictures are:* kitchen, key, kiss; king, ketchup, frank (hot dog); tack, bank, eek; pancake, ski, donkey.*)*

REVIEW   ■

"Tell me some things you learned about counting sounds."

PREVIEW   ■

"Tomorrow, we will finish the short vowel sounds. Does anyone know which vowel we haven't worked on?" *(Take guesses until they identify the /i/ sound.)*

Name _____

Write the number of sounds you hear in each word under the picture. Cut the cards apart. Put them face up in three rows of three. Put the extra three cards in a pile.

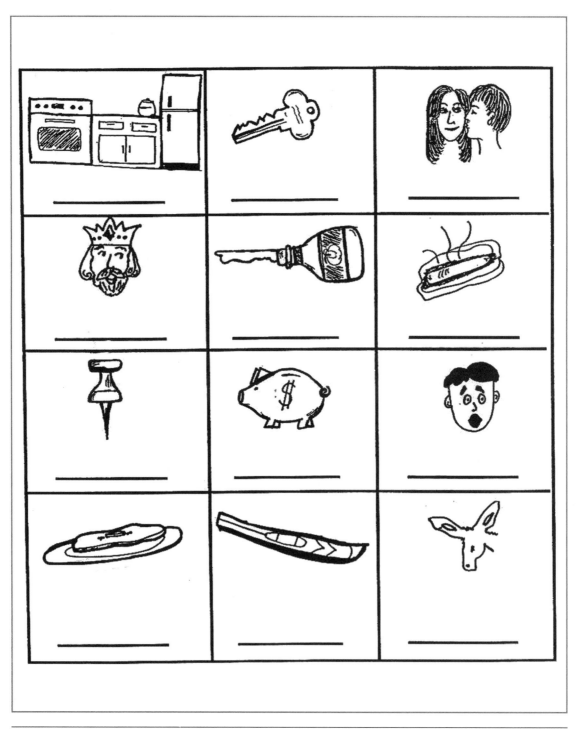

Lesson 33

Segmentation and Identification /i/

OBJECTIVE: Students will be able to count the number of phonemes in words containing the /i/ sound and identify the position of the /i/ phoneme.

MATERIALS: Skittles candies (about 20 for each student)

REVIEW ■

"Who can tell me what we worked with last?" *(Give appropriate feedback, and review any previously mastered content.)*

PREVIEW ■

"Today, we will work with the /i/ sound."

PRESENTATION/INSTRUCTION ■

"Last time, we counted sounds in words and played Bingo. We have worked with the vowels /a/, /o/, /e/, and /u/. The last short vowel we have is /i/. Everyone make the /i/ sound. Let's practice each short vowel sound." *(Review all the vowel sounds, practice saying each phoneme, and talk about the mouth positions for each.)* "Hey, can anyone think of a candy that reminds you of the /i/ sound? I'll give you a hint. The /i/ sound is in the middle." *(Take guesses.)* "Everyone say *Skittles*. We are going to use Skittles to count sounds in words and tell where the /i/ sound is heard. Let me show you how. If I said *kit*, then I stretched it out *kiiiit*, then I said each sound, /k/ /i/ /t/, I could count three sounds." *(Hold up your fingers and say the sounds slowly.)* "On my table, I would put out three Skittles to represent the three sounds. Now if I were to eat the Skittle that stood for the /i/ sound, which one would I eat—the beginning, middle, or end?" *(Say /k/ /i/ /t/ again, holding up fingers.)* "I would eat the middle one, right? Are you ready to try?"

■ GUIDED PRACTICE

"I will pass out the Skittles. Remember, you may eat only one for each word, and I will tell you when to eat. If you follow directions well, we will all finish the Skittles you are given. I'll say the word. You say it slowly and count the sound. Then put out that number of Skittles. Don't eat until we have checked the number. Then we'll eat the /i/ Skittle. Ready, *mint*. How many Skittles?" *(4)* "Which one will you eat?" *(the second one)*

■ INDEPENDENT PRACTICE

"Ready, *Indian*. How many Skittles?" *(5)* "Which one will you eat?" *(the first one) (Repeat the process for:* ribbon *[4],* milk *[4],* fish *[3],* it *[2],* stick *[4],* swim *[4],* lid *[3],* kitten *[4],* igloo *[4],* kid *[3].)*
    "Now let's eat the rest of our Skittles!"

■ REVIEW

"Everyone make the /i/ sound. Terrific! How many sounds in terrific? Six, that is correct."

■ PREVIEW

"We will continue with the /i/ sound tomorrow."

Lesson 34

Comparison /i/

OBJECTIVE: *Students will delete various phonemes in words to make new words.*

MATERIALS: *none*

REVIEW ■

"Who can tell me what sound we worked on yesterday?" *(Give appropriate feedback, and review any previously mastered content.)*

PREVIEW ■

"We are going to continue working on the /i/ sound today."

PRESENTATION/INSTRUCTION ■

"Yesterday, we learned that the /i/ sound makes your mouth stretch sideways. I'd like everyone to make the /i/ sound while I check to see if your mouth position is correct. *(Give individual feedback and correction.)* Great! Now, let's say some /i/ words and stretch out the /i/ sound. Listen carefully as I show you how. The first word is *bridge*. Let's say *br . . . iiiiii . . . dge*. Does everyone see how I did that? Let's try one together. Let's do *swim*. *Sw . . . iiiiii . . . m*. Now let's stretch out the first sound in some words with the /i/ sound in the middle. Let's do *slip*. Ready? *Sssss . . . lip*. If we took off the /s/, what word would be left? Yes, *lip*."

GUIDED PRACTICE ■

"Let's practice listening to two words to find out what is missing in one word. I'll say both words, then I'll ask, 'What's missing?' I'll call on people to tell what they think is missing in one of the words. For example, in *sit* and *it* the only thing different is the /s/ sound on the beginning of *it*. So, you would say /s/ on *it*. Let's do a practice one. Work with your neighbor. *Slid—lid*. What's missing?"

■ INDEPENDENT PRACTICE

(Repeat the same process for the following words.) "I want you to work with a partner. Take turns asking your partner, 'What's missing?'"

pillow—pill	*"What's missing?"*	grim—rim	*"What's missing?"*
stick—tick	*"What's missing?"*	mist—miss	*"What's missing?"*
fit—it	*"What's missing?"*	mink—ink	*"What's missing?"*
fin—in	*"What's missing?"*	pill—ill	*"What's missing?"*
sink—ink	*"What's missing?"*	sister—cyst	*"What's missing?"*
which—itch	*"What's missing?"*	city—sit	*"What's missing?"*
split—slit	*"What's missing?"*	trip—tip	*"What's missing?"*

■ REVIEW

"Today we worked on taking off sounds in words with the /i/ vowel."

■ PREVIEW

"Tomorrow, we play a game with vowel sounds."

Identification of Short Vowels

OBJECTIVE: Students will be able to identify short vowel sounds in words.

MATERIALS: chalkboard, three-minute timer, and Activity Page XX-1 already cut up. (If you are doing this activity with a whole class, you will need Activity Page XX-1 for groups of four to six, with two to three players on each team, and enough timers for each group to have one.)

REVIEW ■

"Who can tell me what vowel sounds we have been working on?" *(Give appropriate feedback, and review any previously mastered content.)*

PREVIEW ■

"Today, we are going to play a game using all of the short vowel sounds."

PRESENTATION/INSTRUCTION ■

"Let's review all the short vowel sounds first. What sound does a short a make?" *(/a/)* "What word do you think of to remember that sound?" *(apple)* "What mouth position does that sound make? Make the /a/ sound while I check your mouth position." *(Repeat the same procedure for /o/, /e/, /u/, and /i/.)*

GUIDED PRACTICE ■

"Let's do one together. Ready? The word has an /a/ sound in the middle." *(Draw a picture to represent* sad *while the students guess. Allow three minutes for guessing or until the correct answer is given.)*

■ INDEPENDENT PRACTICE

"Today we are going to play Picture This Vowel. You will divide up into two teams. Each team will draw a picture card from the pile. One player on the team will look at that picture. That person will tell the vowel sound and draw a picture of the object. If your team guesses the picture within three minutes, your team will get five points. The other team will keep time. Everyone will take turns being the drawer. Remember, the drawer must identify the vowel in each word before he/she starts drawing."

Activity Page XX-1 Picture Key: cup, mop, elf, Eskimos; nap, wet, socks, sun; pot, fan, cap, map; eggs, cuff, shirt, match; fin, fist, masks, bed

■ REVIEW

"Tell me one vowel sound and a word that has that sound."

■ PREVIEW

"Tomorrow we will start work on a new sound!"

Copyright © 2009 by Corwin. All rights reserved. Reprinted from *Phonemic Awareness: Ready-to-Use Lessons, Activities, and Games* by Victoria Groves Scott. Thousand Oaks, CA: Corwin, www.corwinpress.com. Reproduction authorized only for the local school site or nonprofit organization that has purchased this book.

Lesson 36

Identification /l/

OBJECTIVE: Students will identify the /l/ phoneme in initial and final positions in words.

MATERIALS: Activity Page L-1, colors, scissors, and yarn

■ REVIEW

"Who can tell me one sound we have worked on?" *(Give appropriate feedback, and review previously mastered content.)*

■ PREVIEW

"Today, we are going to work with the sound that ends the words *pill, jewel,* and *tool.* What sound ends those words? The /l/ sound!"

■ PRESENTATION/INSTRUCTION

"Everyone make the /l/ sound. Is your mouth closed? *(no)* Are your teeth together? *(no)* Is your mouth open just a little bit? *(yes)* Do you make a puffing sound? *(no)* Does your tongue tap your mouth? *(no)* Is your tongue touching your top teeth? *(yes)* Okay, now everyone make the /l/ sound with your mouth open just a little and your tongue touching the backside of your top teeth. Have your neighbor check your mouth position. This is the position you will look for when you are listening for /l/ sounds in words. Let's see if you can find some."

■ GUIDED PRACTICE

"Listen to these words. I want you to hold your thumb up if you hear the /l/ sound and your thumb down if you don't. The /l/ sound can be in the beginning, middle, or end. Listen carefully: *lemon, tell, fox, like, bottle, star, leaf, puddle, lizard, don't, horse, jewelry, miller, first, lake, lion.*" *(Watch students and give individual correction and feedback.)*

INDEPENDENT PRACTICE ▪

"I am going to give you a lion mask. I would like you to color it and cut it out. Put yarn on each side so you can tie it on your face. On the inside of the mask, draw pictures of all the /l/ words you can think of. When you are done, we are going to use the masks."

(Allow students about 10 minutes to color and draw pictures.)

"Now, I want everyone to put on your lion masks. When you hear the /l/ sound in this poem, you will roar like a lion. Everyone join hands in a big circle. You will sway back and forth as I read and roar when you hear the /l/ sound."

Five Little Lions

Five <u>little</u> <u>lions</u>, <u>sleeping</u> on a <u>log</u>;
One <u>fell</u> off and got <u>lost</u> in the fog.
<u>Linda</u> <u>called</u> the <u>principal</u>, and the <u>principal</u> said,
Make those <u>lions</u> <u>sleep</u> in a bed.

Four <u>little</u> <u>lions</u>, <u>leaping</u> on a <u>log</u>;
One <u>fell</u> off and got <u>lost</u> in the fog.
<u>Lucy</u> <u>called</u> the <u>principal</u>, and the <u>principal</u> said,
Make those <u>lions</u> walk instead.

Three <u>little</u> <u>lions</u>, <u>listening</u> to a <u>log</u>;
One <u>fell</u> down and got <u>lost</u> in the fog.
<u>Larry</u> <u>called</u> the <u>principal</u>, and the <u>principal</u> said,
<u>Let</u> those <u>lions</u> use their heads.

Two <u>little</u> <u>lions</u>, <u>playing</u> on a <u>log</u>;
One <u>fell</u> under and got <u>lost</u> in the fog.
<u>Lyle</u> <u>called</u> the <u>principal</u>, and the <u>principal</u> said,
Send that <u>lion</u> straight to bed.

One <u>little</u> <u>lion</u>, <u>lying</u> all <u>alone</u>;
Ring, ring—the <u>principal's</u> on the phone.
The <u>principal</u> <u>called</u> the <u>lion</u>, and the <u>lion</u> said,
"<u>Let's</u> go out to <u>play</u> on my <u>silly</u> <u>sled</u>!"

(Read slowly the first time, allowing the student to roar with every /l/ word. To save time, you may want the students to roar for the last two or three verses only.)

■ REVIEW

"Tell me one /l/ word you learned today."

■ PREVIEW

"Tomorrow, we will do the /l/ sound again."

 You may want to give older students the first verse of the poem and have them work in groups to create other verses. The lion mask can be used as the cover of a book for their lion poems. The yarn can be used to bind the book.

Lesson 37

Segmentation /l/

OBJECTIVE: Students will count the number of phonemes in words containing the /l/ phoneme.

MATERIALS: pencil, paper, and Activity Page L-2

■ REVIEW

"Who can give me an /l/ word from yesterday?" (*Give appropriate feedback.*)

■ PREVIEW

"Today, we are going to count sounds in words containing the /l/ sound."

■ PRESENTATION/INSTRUCTION

"Let's review the mouth position for the /l/ sound. Who would like to come up and demonstrate? Tell us how our mouths should look. Everyone make the /l/ sound. Check your neighbor to make sure his or her mouth position is correct. Leaping lizards, you guys are great! We are going to count sounds. First, we will say the words in a stretched way. Then, we will pause between each sound, watching for our mouth positions to change. Finally, we will say the word, stopping between sounds while using our fingers to count the sounds. Watch as I demonstrate." (*Say* little. *Stretch the sounds, stop between, then use your fingers.*)

■ GUIDED PRACTICE

"Let's do some together." (*Use the same procedure as above for the words:* ladder, lip, trail, lick, lamp, *and* double. *Talk about the position of the /l/ sound in each word.*)

INDEPENDENT PRACTICE ■

"Now, let's do an activity page. Count the number of sounds in each word. Then write that number below the picture. The pictures are: *lion, owl, lettuce; lantern, volcano, bell; sail, lace, curl; lake, girl, letter.*"

Activity Page L-2 Answer Key

lion–3 (or 4)	owl–2 (or 3)	lettuce–5
lantern–6	volcano–7	bell–3
sail–3	lace–3	curl–3
lake–3	girl–3	letter–4

REVIEW ■

(Check activity page together.) "Lovely work! How many sounds in *lovely*?"

PREVIEW ■

"Tomorrow we will work on a new sound."

A sound-counting relay race might add fun to this lesson. Have the students divide into two teams. The person at the front of the line comes to the chalkboard. The teacher says an /l/ word and the students at the board write the number that corresponds with the phonemes in the word. The first correct answer gets a point.

Words for the relay race:

ladle–4	lather–4	legend–5 (6)	lid–3	lobster–6
lace–3	laundry–6	lemon–5	light–3	low–2
ladder–4	lantern–6	letters–5	liquid–5	lung–3
lake–3	law–2	leave–3	lizard–5	lynx–5
large–3	learn–3	liberty–6	lock–3	lie–2

Name _____

Write the number of sounds you hear in each word under the picture.

Lesson 38

Blending /b/

OBJECTIVE: *Students will delete the initial phoneme in words and blend those phonemes together to form new words.*

MATERIALS: *pencils and Activity Page B-1*

REVIEW ■

"Who can tell me what sound we did yesterday?" *(Give appropriate feedback.)*

PREVIEW ■

"Today, we are going to make /b/ words by blending sounds together."

PRESENTATION/INSTRUCTION ■

"Listen to the /b/ sound. How would you describe that sound?" *(Take comments.)* "Yes, I think it is another puffing sound. Does your tongue go up or down? It stays at the bottom of your mouth. If you make the /b/ sound and move your tongue to the roof of your mouth, what sound would you make? That position makes the /d/ sound. Good problem-solving! Remember, we talked about how blending sounds will help you figure out new words. We learned that you can take sounds and stretch them out. If you run the sounds together, you can hear new words. Listen: /b/ /oo/ /k/, *b . . . oo . . . k*. What word did I make? Yes, *book*."

GUIDED PRACTICE ■

"Now let's try to make some /b/ words. I want three people to come up here and stand in front of the class." *(Pick three students.)* "I will say a word. I want you to remember the beginning sound for your word." *(Point to the first child.)* "Your word is *bear*. Your job is to remember the first sound in the word *bear*." *(Point to the second child.)* "Your word is *ice*. Your job is to remember the first sound in the word *ice*." *(Point to the third child.)* "Your word is *kettle*. Your job is to remember the first sound in the word *kettle*. Let's make a new word." *(Point to each child and have each say his/her sound: /b/ /i/ /k/.)* "If we put those sounds together, /b/ /i/ /k/, what word would we make? *Bike*. That's correct!"

(Continue the same process for the following words.)

cat + rabbit + apple + balloon = *crab*

ball + umbrella + tack + nest = *button*

kitten + astronaut + boy = *cab*

bee + alligator + snake + kite + Indian + tool = *basket*

■ INDEPENDENT PRACTICE

"You get to do an activity page with the same skill. Look at each picture in a row to the left of the line. Say the name of the picture and take off the first sound. Then blend the first sounds together to make a new word. Draw a line to the new word in the column to the right of the line." *(The pictures going across each row are:* bat, elf, leaf, boat; balloon, egg, drum, bee; box, oak, bed; bear, oak, turtle, bow; button, eagle, bell.)

■ REVIEW

(Check activity page together.)

Activity Page B-1 Answer Key

Row 1: *bell*

Row 2: *bed*

Row 3: *bow*

Row 4: *boat*

Row 5: *bee*

"Blend this word: /b/ /e/ /u/ /t/ /i/ /f/ /l/. What word did you make? *Beautiful!*"

■ PREVIEW

"Tomorrow we will play a /b/ game."

Name _____

Say the picture names. Take off the first sound in each picture going across each row to the left of the line. Blend those sounds together to make a new word. Draw a line to the picture of the new word in the column to the right of the line.

Activity Page B-1

Recall and Segmentation /b/

OBJECTIVE: Students will recall words with the /b/ phoneme and give the number of phonemes in each word.

MATERIALS: library books or textbooks with pictures, paper (cut in a circle like a ball), pencil, and a beach ball (or other type of soft ball)

■ REVIEW

"Who can tell me what sound ends the words *cab, crib,* and *web?* It's the sound we worked on yesterday."

■ PREVIEW

"Today, we are going to play a game with the /b/ sound."

■ PRESENTATION/INSTRUCTION

"I would like you to break up into groups of two. Take turns making the /b/ sound, while the other person describes the mouth position. Then switch roles." *(Call on several groups to demonstrate.)* "What did we learn about the /b/ sound yesterday?" *(Take comments.)* "There are lots of words that begin and end with the /b/ sound. We are going to find /b/ words today and count the sounds in those words. Let's review how to count sounds. First you say the word the stretched way. Then, you watch for mouth position changes and stop between sounds. Finally, you use your fingers to count the sounds." *(Demonstrate counting the sounds in the word box.)*

■ GUIDED PRACTICE

"I want everyone to get a book from the shelf. Look through the book and stop on a page that has a picture of a /b/ word. Not the written word, the picture." *(Have the students tell their word while other students count the sounds. Remember, some of the words are tricky to count but it is more important that students think about the number of sounds and listen to the words, than get the correct number. The number of sounds in some words depends on dialect and pronunciation.)* "I want you to continue to look through the books and draw pictures of /b/ words on your paper." *(Paper is cut to look like a ball.)* "Count the number of sounds in your words, and write that number next to the picture. The word can begin or end with /b/ or have the /b/ sound in the middle of it. Work quickly so we have time to play a game." *(Give about 10 minutes to complete this task.)*

INDEPENDENT PRACTICE ■

"I want everyone to sit on their desks. I am going to toss this ball around, and the first person that catches it will say a /b/ word and throw it to someone else. That person will tell the number of sounds in the word just said. Then he/she will throw the ball to someone else to say a /b/ word. Put your pictures near you in case you can't remember a /b/ word." *(If you can, make two or three groups, so students don't wait long between turns.)*

REVIEW ■

"Tell me one /b/ word you found today."

PREVIEW ■

"Tomorrow, we will work with a new sound."

Segmentation and Identification of Long Vowels

OBJECTIVE: *Students will draw circles for each phoneme heard in a word, then fill in the circle for certain phonemes. All of the words will contain long vowels.*

MATERIALS: *pencil, paper, and colors*

■ REVIEW

"Who would like to share two /b/ words you remember from yesterday?"

■ PREVIEW

"Today, we are going to listen for long vowels in words."

■ PRESENTATION/INSTRUCTION

"Long vowels are the vowels a, e, i, o, and u, which say their names. As long as you can remember the letter names, you know the sound! Isn't that easy? I can remember all of my long vowel sounds if I can remember the sentence: Apes Eat Ice Over You! Let's all think for a moment about those apes. If they were over you, where might they be?" *(Take comments.)* "What kind of day do you think it would be if they were eating ice?" *(Take comments.)* "What might the ice be doing on you?" *(Take comments.)* "How would you feel?" *(Take comments.)* "Let's all say 'A, E, I, O, U.' What does your mouth position look like for each?" *(Compare and contrast mouth positions for each.)* "I am going to pass out paper, and I want you to draw a picture of Apes Eating Ice Over You. You seem ready to practice stretching out long-vowel words and counting the sounds. I'll show you first. First, I will say the word in the stretched way. Then, we will hold up our fingers to count the number of sounds we hear. The first word is *tape.* Stretch it out: *taaaap.* Now use your fingers: /t/" *(hold up one finger)* "/a/" *(hold up two fingers)* "/p/" *(hold up three fingers).* "How many sounds in *tape?* Three!"

GUIDED PRACTICE ■

Use the same procedure to do the following words with students: *mule, eat, hope, ride, ape.*

INDEPENDENT PRACTICE ■

"Now, I want you to use the back of your paper. I will say a word. You lis-ten to that word and draw a circle on your paper for each sound you hear. Then fill in the circle for the long vowel." (*Demonstrate on the board for the word made. Remind students that a vowel followed by* r *is counted as one sound.*)

1. boat	○ ● ○	6. sky	○ ○ ●
2. beave	○ ● ○ ○	7. plate	○ ○ ● ○
3. music	○ ● ○ ○ ○	9. east	● ○ ○
4. ate	● ○	10. coach	○ ● ○
5. unicorn	● ○ ○ ○ ○	10. butterfly	○ ○ ○ ○ ○ ○ ●

REVIEW ■

(*Check papers together, and discuss which long vowel was present and the position of the vowel in each word. Display pictures to reinforce retention of the mnemonic.*)

PREVIEW ■

"Tomorrow, we will work with a new sound."

Identification /j/ /v/

OBJECTIVE: *Students will identify the /j/ and /v/ phonemes in initial and final positions in words.*

MATERIALS: *pencils; magazines, scissors, glue, and domino game pattern for enrichment activity; colors; and Activity Page JV-1*

■ REVIEW

"Who can tell me what long vowels are? What's the sentence we use to remember long vowel sounds?" *(Review mouth positions, and give appropriate feedback.)*

■ PREVIEW

"Today, we are going to work with two sounds. The first one begins the word *job*. What sound is that? The second one ends the word *shave*. What sound is that?"

■ PRESENTATION/INSTRUCTION

"Everyone make the /j/ sound. Now, make the /v/ sound. *(Draw a Venn diagram and compare and contrast the two sounds: /j/—tongue touches the ridge in the top of the mouth and taps back of upper teeth, lips purse. /v/—tongue goes down, lips in small oval. Both make a puffing action.)* I want you to turn to your neighbor and make the mouth shape for either /v/ or /j/ . . . *but* don't make the sound. Your neighbor will guess what sound you are making without hearing the sound. Take turns until you each have made both sounds." *(Give feedback to individuals.)* "Is it easy to tell what sound would come out of the mouth from just the mouth position?"

■ GUIDED PRACTICE

"Let's listen to a story that has lots of /v/ and /j/ words. Some of the words begin with the /v/ or /j/ sound and some end with the /v/ or /j/ sound. I want you to make a tally mark on your paper every time you hear either the /v/ or /j/ sound. Draw a line down the middle of the paper.

Draw a valentine at the top on one side and a jet at the top of the other side. Under the valentine, you will mark every time you hear a /v/ sound. Under the jet, you will mark every time you hear a /j/ sound. Draw a line under the tally mark if the /j/ or /v/ comes at the beginning of the word. Let me show you how. Suppose I say, "<u>J</u>ack wants some <u>of</u> the <u>v</u>egetables in that <u>jar</u>." You will put two tallies under the jet and underline both and two tallies under the valentine. The second one would be underlined." *(Do this on the board to model steps.)* "Did the word *of* trick anyone? Listen carefully!"

Julie the Veterinarian

<u>J</u>ulie is a <u>v</u>eterinarian. It's her <u>j</u>ob to <u>v</u>accinate <u>v</u>ery fine animals. The dogs <u>behave</u> and don't <u>jump</u> or <u>jiggle</u>, because she will <u>give</u> them <u>fudge</u> treats and <u>juice</u>. The cats <u>just</u> move and <u>jolt</u>. They like <u>J</u>ulie, but they don't eat <u>fudge</u>.

(Now go through the story slowly and identify each /j/ or /v/ sound and its position in the word—beginning or end.)

INDEPENDENT PRACTICE ■

"We are going to do an activity page. All of the words either begin or end with either the /j/ or /v/ sound. You will paste the jet nose under the picture if it *begins* with /j/ or /v/ and paste the jet tail under the picture if it *ends* with the /j/ or /v/ sound. If the first picture was of a cave, what would you paste under the picture? The jet tail, because the word *cave* ends with the /v/ sound. If the picture was of a vacuum, what picture would you paste? The jet nose, because *vacuum* begins with the /v/ sound. Then go back and color all the jet parts that are under pictures that have the /j/ sound in them. Do you have any questions? Put your finger on the picture as I say it: *volcano, jar, wave; hive, hinge, jack-o-lantern.*"

REVIEW ■

"Tell me one word that begins or ends with the /j/ sound. Tell me one word that begins or ends with the /v/ sound." *(Give each child the opportunity to give a word. If they can't remember, have another student act out the /j/ word while that students guesses.)*

PREVIEW ■

"Tomorrow, we begin work on two new sounds."

For enrichment, your students could create a game. Have the students look through magazines for pictures that begin and end with either the /j/ or /v/ sound. Glue the pictures on domino patterns. The students must link pictures that begin the same, have the same number of sounds, or have the same ending sounds. You can decide the difficulty of the game. The teacher will have to check the game to be sure the pictures are correct and that the domino pieces can be matched. Picture cutting is an excellent phonemic awareness activity.

Domino Game Pattern

Laminate the cards after the pictures are glued on for durability.

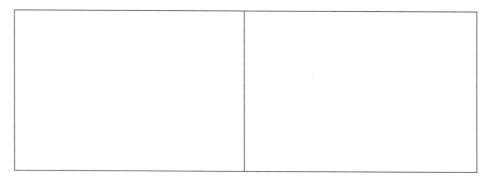

Name _____

Cut out the pictures of the jet nose and tail at the bottom of the page. Paste the jet nose under the pictures that begin with /j/ or /v/. Paste the jet tail under pictures that end with /j/ or /v/. Now go back and color each picture that has the /j/ sound in it.

Activity Page JV-1

Blending /g/ /y/

OBJECTIVE: Students will blend individual phonemes together to form words with the /g/ and /y/ phonemes.

MATERIALS: scissors and Activity Page GY-1

■ REVIEW

"Who can tell me what sounds we worked on yesterday?" (*Give appropriate feedback.*)

■ PREVIEW

"We are going to do two sounds again today. The sounds are /g/ and /y/."

■ PRESENTATION/INSTRUCTION

"The /g/ and /y/ sounds are both sounds that make a puffing action inside your mouth. Everyone make the /g/ sound. Now make the /y/ sound. Did you feel the puffs of air inside your mouth? Can you make the /g/ sound and /y/ sound without moving your lips? Yes, you can. Can you make the /y/ sound without moving your mouth? No. See how different the /g/ and /y/ are from that puffing sound? The /g/ and /y/ only puff air on the inside without moving your lips. How can we tell the sounds apart if the mouth positions are so much the same? We can also remember key words for each sound. I remember the word *yawn* for the /y/ sound, because /y/ is such a lazy sound that your lips don't have to move much, and the word *yawn* makes me think of lazy days. What do you do on your lazy days? I think of the word *gas* for the /g/ sound, because the /g/ sound looks like your lips are running out of gas. Now let's try making some words with those two sounds. I'll say the sounds, and you blend the sounds to make a word. Ready? /g/ /ar/ /d/ /n/ = What?" (*Pronounce the individual sounds.*) "That's right, *garden*. What sound did you hear /g/ or /y/? Was it at the beginning or end of the word?"

GUIDED PRACTICE ■

"Let's see if you can solve some blending mysteries. What word am I saying? /y/ /a/ /m/. Everyone . . . *yam.* What sound did you hear, /g/ or /y/? Was it at the beginning or end of the word?" *(Say the sounds separately, and have the students blend the sounds and call out the word. Blend the words:* gift, bug, yak, yell, game, yarn.*)*

INDEPENDENT PRACTICE ■

"Now, let's play a Blend-O game. I am going to give you a sheet of paper with pictures. Cut out the pictures, and place nine of them in front of you in three rows of three. You will have leftover cards. Stack them and put them on the corner of your desk. I will say sounds, and you will blend those sounds together to make a new word. Find the picture of that new word, and turn the picture over. When you get three in a row (across, up and down, or diagonally), yell out 'Blend-O!' You must then say the words back so I can check your three in a row. Now, let's go over the pictures so you know what they stand for. Look at the sheet I am passing out. Put your finger on the picture as I say it. The pictures are: *girl, globe, golf; grapes, game, glasses; bug, log, yardstick; yo-yo, yarn, yolk."* *(Make an extra set for yourself, and pronounce the words, phoneme by phoneme.)*

REVIEW ■

"What two sounds did we work on today?"

PREVIEW ■

"Tomorrow, we will do two new sounds."

Cut the cards apart. Lay them out, face up, in three rows of three. Put the extra cards in a pile.

Rhyming of Long Vowels

OBJECTIVE: *Students will be able to identify rhyming words containing long vowel sounds.*

MATERIALS: *scissors and Activity Pages XX-2*

REVIEW ■

"Who can name all the vowels for me?" *(Give appropriate feedback.)*

PREVIEW ■

"We are going to work on long vowel sounds to make rhymes."

PRESENTATION/INSTRUCTION ■

"Long vowels are sounds that say their letter names. Everyone make the sounds 'A, E, I, O, U.' Who can remember the sentence we use to help us remember long vowels? 'Apes eat ice over you' is the sentence to remember long vowel sounds. See how the mouth position changes for the different sounds? Now, let's see if we can make some rhyming words with long vowel sounds. Remember that a rhyme is a sound pattern. Who can share some patterns?" *(Take comments.)* "To rhyme, you take off the beginning sound, keep the vowel and the rest of the word, and change the beginning sound. In the word *rain*, what's the beginning sound? It's /r/. Take off the /r/, and what is left? . . . *ain*. If I put a /tr/ on the beginning of *ain*, I'd make the word *train*."

GUIDED PRACTICE ■

"Let's go through the alphabet and see if we can add other sounds at the beginning of *ain* to make new words." *(Have the students say the sounds associated with each letter of the alphabet and decide if, when added to* ain*, it makes a new word.)*

■ INDEPENDENT PRACTICE

"I am going to read a poem. It has some long vowel rhyming words. See if you can find them."

Little Bo Peep

Little Bo Peep has lost her sheep,

And can't tell where to find them;

Leave them alone, and they'll come home,

Wagging their tails behind them.

(Identify the long vowel words and all the long vowel rhyming words.)
"Let's play a game with the long vowel sounds. You will play in groups of three. First cut the cards apart. Then you will shuffle the cards and give out nine cards to each player. You must get three rhyming cards to make a book. When you get a book, you lay your book on the table. To get a book, you ask the other players, 'Do you have a card that rhymes with . . .?' If they do, they must give all rhyming cards to the person that asks. If not, they draw a card from that player's hand. When all the cards are in books, the game is over."
(Go through the pictures, name the cards, and discuss the rhyming words and the vowel sounds. Pictures: bead, seed, read; meat, feet, eat; bone, cone, phone; coat, boat, goat; nose, rose, hose; lace, face, race; nail, tail, pail; five, hive, dive; fin, in, pin.)

■ REVIEW

"Who can tell me a word that rhymes with cute?" *(fruit, boot, suit, etc.)*

■ PREVIEW

"Tomorrow, we will work with two new sounds."

Activity Page XX-2a

Deletion /h/ /w/

OBJECTIVE: Students will be able to delete initial phonemes in words with /h/ and /w/ phonemes to make new words.

MATERIALS: scissors and Activity Pages HW-1

■ REVIEW

"Who can tell me what we worked on yesterday?" (*Give appropriate feedback, and review any previously mastered content.*)

■ PREVIEW

"Today, we are going to work with the sounds /h/ and /w/."

■ PRESENTATION/INSTRUCTION

"Listen carefully: /h/. Who can describe that sound?" (*It's a puffing sound. Your lips don't move.*) Now listen: /w/. Who can describe that sound?" (*It is a puffing sound. Your lips do move.*) "Tell me some words that begin with the /h/ sound. Now, let's see if we can take the first sound off of some words. Who remembers how to do that?"

(*Say the word the stretched way, watch for mouth position changes, stop after you say the first sound, then say the rest of the word.*) "If you take off the /w/ in *wake*, what word is left? If you take off the /h/ in *hat*, what word is left?"

■ GUIDED PRACTICE

(*Continue the process above to delete the initial phoneme in the words:* wind, had, hair, water, *and* his.)

■ INDEPENDENT PRACTICE

"Now, let's play a game. In this game, you will find matches, just as in Memory or Concentration. I will give you a set of cards. You will turn the cards over. If the card starts with a /h/ or a /w/ sound, you take off that sound and try to find the picture of the word that is left. If the picture does not start with a /h/ or a /w/ sound, you will add the sound that makes a real word and look for that picture. Each player takes turns turning over two cards. If you get a match, you keep the cards and get another turn. You will play until all the cards are gone. Let's do one together. If I turned over a picture of an ax, does it begin with /h/ or /w/? No, so add a /h/ to ax. Does that make a word? (Hax, *take appropriate answers.*) Add a /w/ to ax. Does that make a word? (Wax, *take appropriate answers.*) So the pictures of the wax and the ax are matches. The pictures are: eat, howl, owl; heel, wind, end (of the rainbow); eel, water, otter; heart, art, hare; hear, ear, air; wax, ax, and heat. Let's see if we can find the matches before we start the game. Remember that the words are the same word without a /h/ or /w/ at the beginning. (*heat–eat, howl–owl, heel–eel, wind–end, water–otter, heart–art, hare–air, hear–ear, wax–ax*)

"Hey, what do all of these word pairs have in common? That's right; they rhyme! Let's play."

REVIEW   ■

(*Review the matches for the game.*) "Tell me one thing you learned today."

PREVIEW   ■

"Tomorrow, we will work with two new sounds."

Activity Page HW-1a

Identification /z/ /qu/

OBJECTIVE: Students will be able to identify the /z/ and /qu/ phoneme in words.

MATERIALS: chalkboard, a three-minute timer, and Activity Pages ZQU-1
(already cut up. If you are doing this activity with a whole class, you will
need: Activity Page ZQU-1 for groups of four to six, two to three players
on each team, and enough timers for each group to have one).

■ REVIEW

"Who can tell me what sound we worked on last?" (*Give appropriate feedback.*)

■ PREVIEW

"Today, we are going to play a game with the /z/ and /qu/ sounds."

■ PRESENTATION/INSTRUCTION

"Listen to the /z/ sound. What does that sound make you think of?" (*a
bee*) "What mouth position does that sound make? Do you think it is a
puffing sound? No, I don't think so either. The /z/ sound is a sound that
is a lip cooler. It cools your lip by pushing air across your bottom lip. Okay,
make the /qu/ sound. Is that the same type of sound? No, it is a puffing
sound. It makes me think of a duck because the word *quack* begins with the
/qu/ sound, and my lips move in a position like they are trying to make a
duck's bill. Make the /z/ sound while I check your mouth position. Great,
now make the /qu/ sound while I check your mouth position. I'll say a
word, and we will decide if it has the /qu/ or /z/ sound. If it makes the
/qu/ sound, I want you to quack. If it makes the /z/ sound, I want you to
buzz like a bee. For the word *quick*, I would quack, and for the word *xylophone*, I would buzz." (*Instead of buzzing and quacking, you could have them
hold up a picture of a duck or bee.*)

GUIDED PRACTICE ■

"Let's do some together. Ready?" (*Say the words:* quarrel, zap, quart, quiz, *and* zone, *and have the students quack or buzz.*) "Now, I will draw a picture. I want you to guess the word. It begins with a /qu/ sound. Ready?" (*Draw a picture to represent* quarrel. *Allow three minutes for guessing or until the correct answer is given.*)

INDEPENDENT PRACTICE ■

"Today, we are going to play Picture That Sound. You will divide up into two teams. Each team will draw a picture card from the pile. One player on the team will look at that picture. That person will tell whether the word starts with /z/ or /qu/ and draw a picture of the object on the chalkboard. If your team guesses the picture within three minutes, then your team will get five points. The other team will keep time. Everyone will take turns being the drawer. Remember the drawer must identify the initial sound in each word before he/she starts drawing. (*The pictures are:* question, queen, quilt; quail, quack, quarter; quiet, zero, zipper; zip code, zebra, zigzag; quote, quick, quiz; zoo, quake, xylophone.)

REVIEW ■

"Tell me one word that has the /qu/ sound." (*Take comments.*) "Tell me one word that has the /z/ sound." (*Take comments.*)

PREVIEW ■

"Tomorrow, we will work with long vowels again! Who can name the long vowels?"

Activity Page ZQU-1a

Activity Page ZQU-1b

Segmentation of Long Vowels

OBJECTIVE: *Students will be able to count the number of sounds heard in words containing long vowel sounds.*

MATERIALS: *pencils and Activity Page XX-5*

■ REVIEW

"Who can tell me what sentence we remember for long vowel sounds? What sound does the long vowel make? Yes, it says its name. Everyone say the vowels with me: A, E, I, O, U."

■ PREVIEW

"Today, we are going to count sounds in words that have long vowels."

■ PRESENTATION/INSTRUCTION

"Remember, we found out that some words have a lot of sounds, and some words have only a few. When you say a word, if you listen carefully you can hear all the sounds in the word. If I say the word *lake* slowly, *llllaaaak*, *llll . . . aaaa . . . k*, I hear three sounds. I hear /l/" *(hold up one finger)*, "/a/" *(hold up two fingers)*, "/k/" *(hold up three fingers)*. "It is important to think only about the sounds in the word, because if you think of the number of letters, you might get the wrong answer." *(Write the word* rain *on the board.)* "What is this word? Everyone say the word *rain*. Now stretch it out. Hold up that many fingers. Everyone who has three fingers up is correct. The word *rain* has only three sounds, but it has four letters. Most of the time, it takes two letters to make a vowel long. Who can tell me two ways to spell words with long vowels? One is with a silent *e* on the end, such as *pine*, and the other is two vowels next to each other such as *neat*. Remember to listen, and don't think about the spelling."

GUIDED PRACTICE ■

"Let's do some words together, and first say them the stretched way. Then, we will hold up our fingers to count the number of sounds we hear. Ready? The first word is *ape*. Stretch it out: *aaaap*. Now use your fingers: /â/ /p/." *(Hold up fingers as you say the sounds.)* "How many sounds in *ape*? Two!" *(Use the same procedure to do the following words:* easy, mule, grapes, ice, hope.)

INDEPENDENT PRACTICE ■

"Now we are going to do a sound-counting activity page. Let's go through the pictures. After I name the pictures, you will say the picture's name and count the sounds. Write the number of sounds under the picture on the line. The pictures are: train, loaf, tie; peek, unicorn, table; pineapple, grapes, and beak."

REVIEW ■

(Check the activity page together.) "Who counted all of the sounds correctly? Great work!"

PREVIEW ■

"Tomorrow, we will work on a new sound. The sound starts the word *shoe*. What sound is that? Yes, we will work on the /sh/ sound tomorrow."

Name _____

Write the number of sounds you hear in each word under the picture.

Activity Page xx-5

Lesson 47

Identification /sh/

OBJECTIVE: Students will be able to identify the /sh/ sound in words.

MATERIALS: crayons, shark puppet (optional), and Activity Page SH-1

REVIEW ■

"Listen to the word *shave*. What sound do you hear at the beginning of the word *shave*? Do you hear a /s/ sound? Do you hear a /h/ sound? No, that's because when the *s* and *h* letters come next to each other, they make only one sound. They say /sh/."

PREVIEW ■

"Today, we are going to learn about the /sh/ sound."

PRESENTATION/INSTRUCTION ■

"Look at my mouth position." *(Say /s/, then say /h/.)* "Who can describe my mouth position for the two sounds." *(Take comments.)* "Now watch: /sh/. Did you see or hear the /s/ sound or the /h/ sound? No, but the /sh/ sound is spelled with the letters *s* and *h*. When these two letters stand next to each other in a word, they make a sound that is different than both of the letters. They make the /sh/ sound. Everyone make the /sh/ sound. Who can describe the mouth position for the /sh/ sound? What does that sound remind you of?" *(someone telling you to be quiet)*

GUIDED PRACTICE ■

"Let's listen to some words. Put your thumb up when you hear the /sh/ sound." *(Say the following words, waiting for the students to put their thumbs up after the /sh/ words: sheet, sit, shovel, heart, shelf, dress, sock, shave.)*
    "Now, I am going to read you a story. I want you to put a tally mark on your paper every time you hear a /sh/ sound." *(Use the back of the activity page.)*

Shelly the Shark

Shelly the shark was sort of short. Being short made Shelly shy. Shelly would swim in the shallow water near the shore to stay away from the other fish. One day, Shelly met a shad named Sherman. "What a shame it is that you are so shy," said Sherman. "You may be short, but you are surely a shiny, shimmery shark." After that, Shelly left the shallow water and swam proudly with the other fish.

(Review the story and identify the /sh/ words together. Count the /sh/ sounds and compare to their tally marks.)

 INDEPENDENT PRACTICE

"I am going to give you an activity page with pictures on it. I want you to color all the pictures that have a /sh/ sound in them. The pictures are: *shoe, shark, star, snake, sheep,* and *shell.*"

■ **REVIEW**

(Correct activity page together.) "What sound did we work on today? How many letters spell /sh/? What are the two letters?"

■ **PREVIEW**

"Great! Tomorrow, we will continue with the /sh/ sound."

Name _____

Color all the pictures that begin with the /sh/ sound.

Activity Page SH-1

Lesson 48

Segmentation /sh/

OBJECTIVE: *Students will count the number of sounds in words containing the /sh/ phoneme.*

MATERIALS: *folders (one for every four students), gray construction paper, (optional colored paper for shark markers), tagboard, glue, scissors, brass fasteners, and Activity Pages SH-2*

■ REVIEW

"Who can tell me what sound we worked on yesterday?"

■ PREVIEW

"Today, we will play a game with the /sh/ sound."

■ PRESENTATION/INSTRUCTION

"What two letters spell the /sh/ sound? That's right the letter *s* and the letter *h*. Do you hear the /s/ and the /h/ in the sound /sh/? No, when the letters *s* and *h* come next to each other, they make a new sound—only one sound. We will count the sounds in some /sh/ words. Who can tell me how to count sounds?" *(Say the word the stretched way, stop between sounds, watch for mouth position changes, put a finger up for each sound.)* "Let me do one for you." *(Demonstrate sound counting for the words* shell *and* fish.)

■ GUIDED PRACTICE

"Let's count some sounds together." *(Use the same procedure as above to count the sounds in the words:* sheet, shelf, shine, sugar, flash, push, *and* splash.)

■ INDEPENDENT PRACTICE

"Now, we are going to play a board game by counting sounds in words. Some of the words have the /sh/ sound and some do not. You must count

158

the sounds and tell if you hear the /sh/ sound." (*Make folder game using Activity Pages SH-2. You will need one folder game for every four students. Follow the directions on the Activity Pages for construction and rules.*) The pictures are: rush, lash, mash; wish, dish, fish; brush, shell, shark; sheep, shoe, sheriff; shirt, shovel, shave; shot, shower, ship; fan, lizard, book; piano, kettle, vase; apple, kiss, owl; mouth, quarter, zebra; hook, unicorn, kite; sink, jar, van." (*Show pictures.*)

REVIEW ■

"What sound did we work on today? What is special about that sound? (*Two letters spell one sound.*) "How may sounds do you hear in the word *shark*? You have learned all of your consonant sounds, short vowel sounds, and long vowel sounds. How do you think this will help you in reading? What parts did you like the best?"

PREVIEW ■

"Tomorrow, we will. . . ."

Activity

Folder Game: /sh/ shark
(skill: segmentation)

Game parts needed for each game:

- File folder with game board glued onto the inside and gray shark's tail glued onto the top
- Markers to move around the board (one for each player)—these can be any small objects you choose, but each should be different in some way
- One spinner (to be constructed)
- One set of the game cards

Instructions for making game parts:

1. Cut out the shark game board, and glue it onto the inside of the folder.

2. Cut the shark's tail out of gray construction paper, and glue it onto the top of the folder.

3. Gather markers (or make markers by making small sharks out of different colors of construction paper).

4. Copy the spinner board and pointer onto tagboard, and cut them out. Using a brass fastener, loosely fasten the base of the pointer to the middle of the spinner board so that the arrow spins freely.

5. Copy game cards (/sh/ pictures) onto tagboard or colored construction paper, and cut them out.

Rules:

The cards are placed facedown on the board. All the students put their markers at the starting point. The first player spins the spinner and chooses a card from the top of the card pile. The student then says the name of the picture and the number of sounds heard in the word (using his or her fingers to count the sounds). If the student is correct, then he or she moves his or her marker the number of spaces indicated by the spinner. If the student does not identify the correct number of sounds, he or she is not allowed to move the marker forward. Each player takes turns until one player reaches the WINNER space.

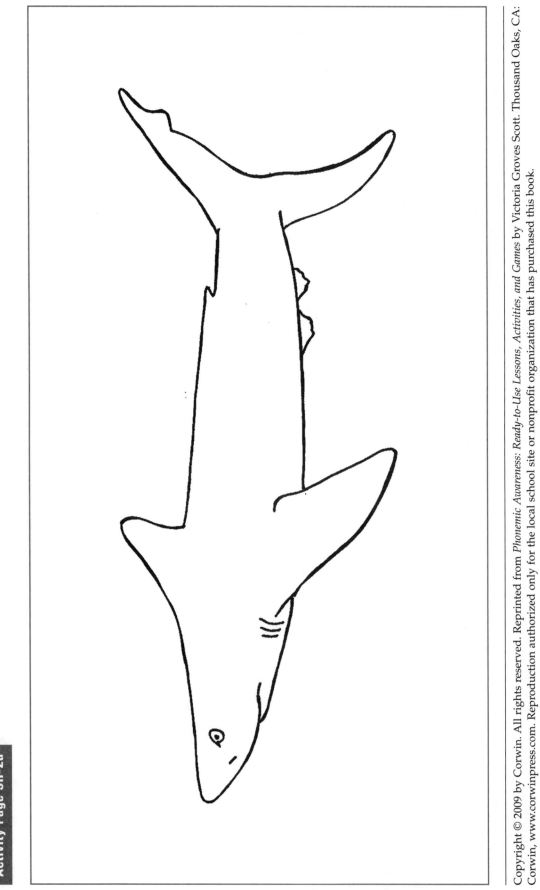

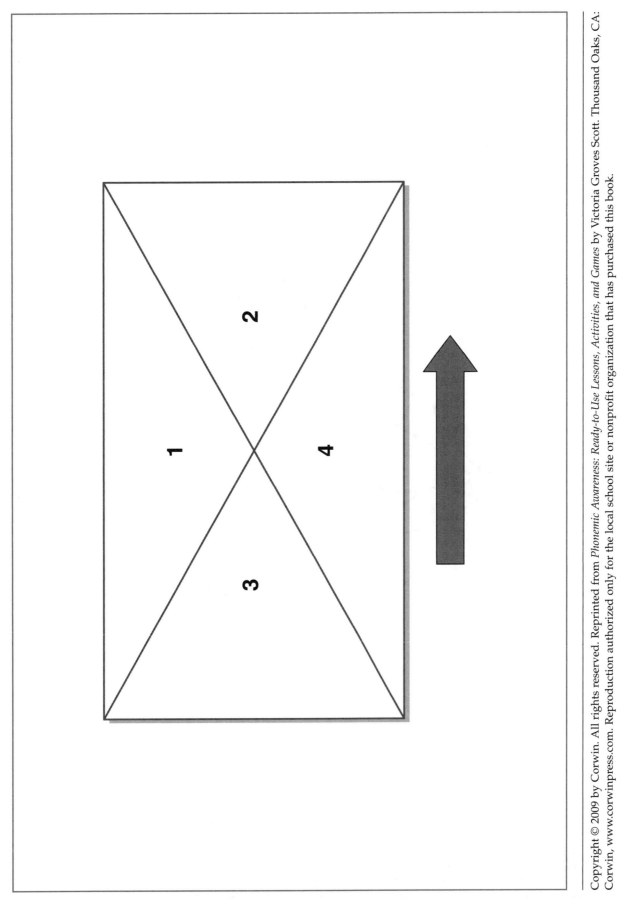

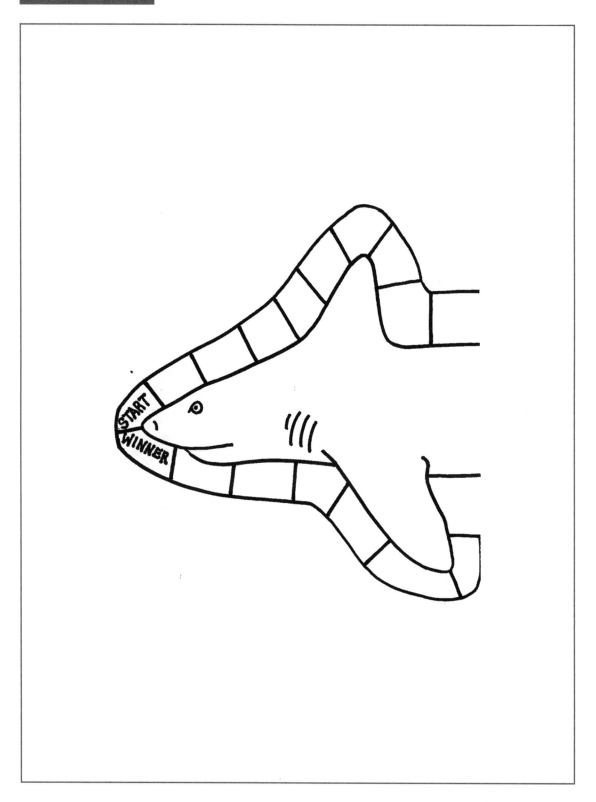

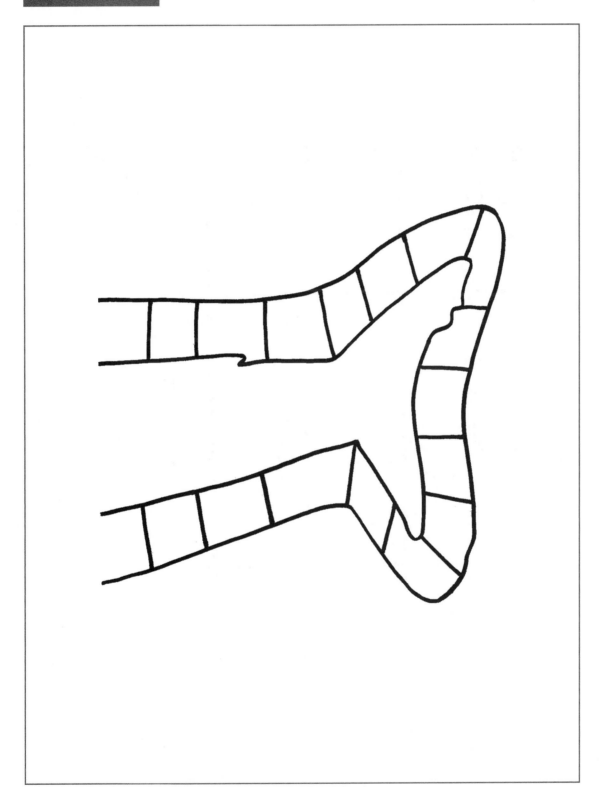

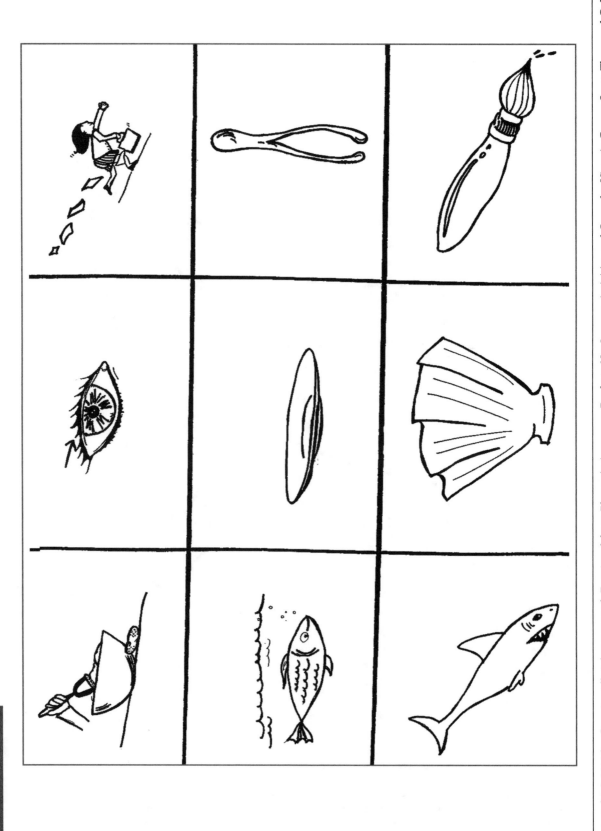

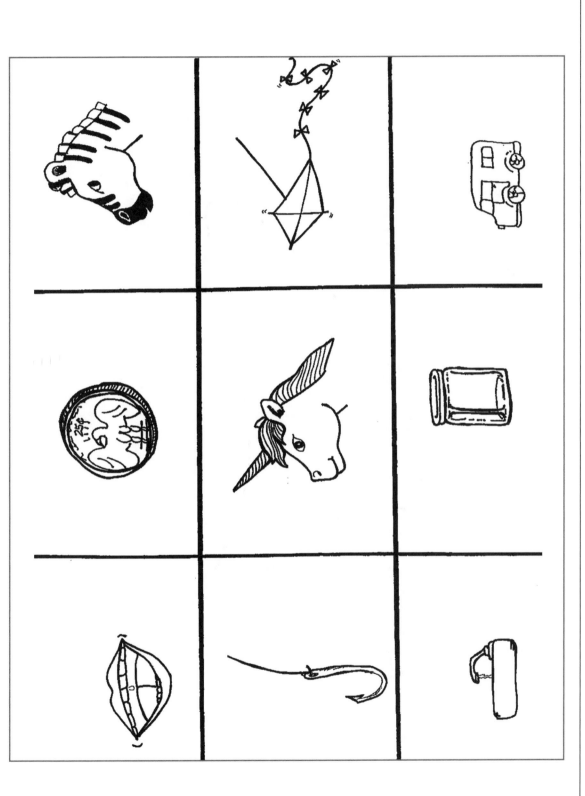

Activity Page SH-2i

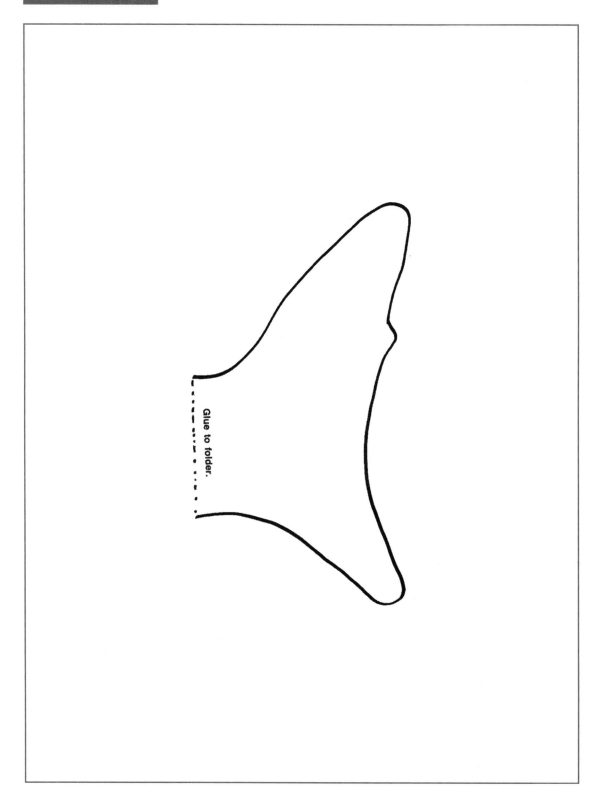

Glue to folder.

I hope you have enjoyed these lessons!

Resource

*Progress Charts and
Lesson Plan Template*

Progress Charts

Table 51.1 Progress Chart Identification of Phonemes

Identification: Using the task "What sound do you hear at the beginning [middle, end] of the word _____?"

Recall: Using the task "Tell me a word that begins [ends] with the sound _____."

Key: + = Identification; ++ = Identification and Recall

Student's Name	/d/	/s/	/a/	/f/	/o/	/m/	/r/	/e/	/p/	/n/	/u/	/t/	/k/	/l/

Phoneme

Table 51.2 Progress Chart Identification of Phonemes

Identification: Using the task "What sound do you hear at the beginning [middle, end] of the word _____?"

Recall: Using the task "Tell me a word that begins [ends] with the sound _____."

Key: + = Identification; ++ = Identification and Recall

Student's Name	Phoneme																		
	/b/	/v/	/j/	/y/	/g/	/h/	/w/	/z/	/gu/	/a/	/e/	/i/	/o/	/u/	/sh/				

Table 51.3 Progress Chart Phonemic Awareness

Segmentation:

Count Phonemes: Using the task "How many sounds do you hear in the word _____?"

Deletion: Using the task "If you take off the /_/ sound [either beginning or end] from the word _____, what word would be left?"

Blending: Using the task "When you put these sounds together, /_/ /_/ /_/, what word would you make?"

Rhyming: Using the task "Tell me another word that rhymes with _____."

Key: Write in date of mastery.

Student's Name	Skills						
	Counts Sounds	Initial Deletion	Final Deletion	Blends 3 Sounds	Blends 4 Sounds	Blends 5 Sounds	Rhyming

Lesson Plan Template					
Sound:					
Skill (circle):	Identification	Segmentation	Blending	Rhyming	Deletion

Objective:

Materials Needed:

Review: (Activate prior knowledge)

Preview: (Tell the students what the lesson will be about)

Presentation: (Define the skills, identify mouth position of sound, model)

Guided Practice: (Practice with the students)

Independent Practice: (Students practice alone)

Review: (Recap the lesson)

Preview: (Tell them what the next lesson will be about)

References

Ackerman, P. T., & Dykman R. A. (1993). Phonological processes, confrontational naming, and immediate memory in dyslexia. *Journal of Learning Disabilities, 26,* 597–609.

Adams, M. J., & Henry, M. K. (1997). Myths and realities about words and literacy. *School Psychology Review, 26,* 425–436.

Alexander, A. W., Andersen, H. G., Heilman, P. C., Voller, K. S., & Torgesen, J. K. (1991). Phonological awareness training and remediation of analytic decoding deficits in a group of severe dyslexics. *Annals of Dyslexia, 41,* 193–206.

Anthony, J. L., & Francis, D. (2005). Development of phonological awareness. *Current Directions in Psychological Science, 14,* 255–259.

Anthony, J. L., Williams, J. M., McDonald, R., & Francis, D. (2007). Phonological processing and emergent literacy in younger and older preschool children. *Annals of Dyslexia, 57,* 113–137.

Ball, E. W., & Blachman, B. A. (1991). Does phoneme awareness training in kindergarten make a difference in early word recognition and developmental spelling? *Reading Research Quarterly, 26*(1), 49–66.

Blachman, B. A. (1991). Early intervention for children's reading problems: Clinical applications of the research in phonological awareness. *Topics in Language Disorders, 1,* 51–63.

Brennan, F., & Ireson, J. (1997). Training phonological awareness: A study to evaluate the effects of a program of metalinguistic games in kindergarten. *Reading and Writing: An Interdisciplinary Journal, 9,* 241–263.

Bryant, P. E. (1990). Rhyme and alliteration, phoneme detection, and learning to read. *Developmental Psychology, 26*(3), 429–438.

Bryant, P. E., Bradley, L., MacLean, M., & Crossland, J. (1989). Nursery rhymes, phonological skills and reading. *Journal of Child Language, 16,* 407–428.

Bryant, P. E., MacLean, M., Bradley, L., & Crossland, J. (1989). Rhyme and alliteration, phoneme deletions, and learning to read. *Developmental Psychology, 26,* 429–438.

Bryne, B., & Fielding-Barnsly, R. (1991). Evaluation of a program to teach phonemic awareness to young children. *Journal of Educational Psychology, 83,* 451–455.

Catts, H. W. (1986). Speech production/phonological deficits in reading-disordered children. *Journal of Learning Disabilities, 19*(8), 504–508.

Catts, H. W. (1991). Facilitation of phonological awareness: Role of speech-language pathologists. *Language, Speech, and Hearing Services in Schools, 22,* 196–203.

DeJong, P. F. (2007). Phonological awareness and the use of phonological similarity in letter-sound learning. *Journal of Experimental Child Psychology, 98*(3), 131–152.

Ehri, L. C. (2005). Learning to read words: Theory, findings, and issues. *Scientific Studies of Reading, 9*(2), 167–188.

Ehri, L. C., Nunes, S. R., Willows, D. M., Schuster, B. V., Yaghoub-Zadeh, Z., & Shanahan, T. (2001). Phonemic awareness instruction help children learn to read: Evidence for the National Reading Panel's meta-analysis. *Reading Research Quarterly, 36*(3), 250–287.

Gillet, J. W., & Temple, C. (1979). Developing word knowledge: A cognitive view. *Reading World, 18*(2), 132–140.

Hatcher, P. J., Hulme, C., & Ellis, N. (1994). Ameliorating early reading failure by integrating the teaching of reading and phonological skills: The phonological linkage hypothesis. *Child Development, 65*(1), 41–57.

Hunter, M. (1982). *Mastery teaching.* Thousand Oaks, CA: Corwin Press.

Manyak, P. C. (2008). Phonemes in use: Multiple activities for a critical process. *Reading Teacher, 61*(8), 659–662.

Pulakanaho, A., Ahonen, T., Aro, M., Eklund, K., Leppanen, P., Tolvanen, A., et al. (2008). Developmental links of very early phonological and language skills to second grade reading outcomes. *Journal of Learning Disabilities, 41*(4), 353–370.

Scott, V. G. (1995). *The effects of phonological awareness training on word recognition and decoding skills of students with a reading disability.* Published doctoral dissertation, University of Kansas.

Snider, V. E. (1995). Primer on phonemic awareness: What it is, why it's important, and how to teach it. *School Psychology Review, 24*(3), 443–455.

Stanovich, K. E. (1988). The right and wrong places to look for the cognitive locus of reading disability. *Annals of Dyslexia, 38,* 154–177.

Stuart, M., & Masterson, J. (1992). Patterns of reading and spelling in 10-year-old children related to prereading phonological abilities. *Journal of Experimental Child Psychology, 54,* 168–187.

Swank, L. K., & Catts, H. W. (1991). *Phonological awareness.* Paper presented at the annual meeting of the International Reading Association, Las Vegas, NV. (ERIC Document Reproduction Service No. ED335663)

Temple, C., & Gillet, J. (1989). *Language arts: Learning processes and training practices.* Glenview, IL: Scott Foresman.

Torgesen, J. K., Morgan, S. T., & Davis, C. (1992). Effects of two types of phonological awareness training on word learning in kindergarten children. *Journal of Educational Psychology, 84,* 3, 364–370.

Torppa, M., Poikkeus, A., Laakso, M., Eklund, K., & Lyytinen, H. (2006). Predicting delayed letter knowledge development and its relation to Grade 1 reading achievement among children with and without familial risk for dyslexia. *Developmental Psychology, 42,* 1128–1142.

Wagner, R.K., Torgeson, J.K., & Rashotte, C. A. (1994). Development of reading-related phonological processing abilities: New evidence of bidirectional causality from a latent variable longitudinal study. *Developmental Psychology, 30,* 73–87.

Yopp, H. K. (1992). Developing phonemic awareness in young children. *The Reading Teacher, 45*(3), 696–703.

Index